The Fourth Tier

PREVIOUS BOOKS BY CHRISTOPHER COLWELL

*Impact: How Assistant Principals
Can Be High Performing Leaders*
(Rowman & Littlefield, March 2015)

*Mission-Driven Leadership:
Understanding the Challenges Facing Schools Today*
(Rowman & Littlefield, March 2018)

The Fourth Tier

Leadership and
the Power of Charisma

Christopher Colwell

ROWMAN & LITTLEFIELD
Lanham • Boulder • New York • London

Published by Rowman & Littlefield
An imprint of The Rowman & Littlefield Publishing Group, Inc.
4501 Forbes Boulevard, Suite 200, Lanham, Maryland 20706
www.rowman.com

6 Tinworth Street, London SE11 5AL, United Kingdom

British Library Cataloguing in Publication Information Available

Library of Congress Cataloging-in-Publication Data

ISBN 9781475850581 (cloth : alk. paper)
ISBN 9781475850598 (pbk : alk. paper)
ISBN 9781475850604 (electronic)

∞™ The paper used in this publication meets the minimum requirements of American National Standard for Information Sciences—Permanence of Paper for Printed Library Materials, ANSI/NISO Z39.48-1992.

To Monique
My Beautiful Bride

Contents

PART III: CHARISMATIC LEADERSHIP IN ACTION

Foreword

Imagine for a moment what set of skills and attributes you believe a twenty-first-century school leader should have in order to be an effective leader. Furthermore, imagine how those skills and attributes may lend themselves to ensuring that all students, regardless of their demographics, are college, career, and life ready in this day and age. In reflecting on the skills and attributes you have identified, now consider the societal expectations that come with leading a school district (superintendency) or school building (principalship) in the twenty-first century.

As many of you may have imagined, leading schools in today's world is very different from leading schools in the past, and, perhaps worth noting, not so distant past. The days of superintendents and principals being just great managers of daily tasks are quickly fading—as twenty-first-century school leaders must also be instructional leaders, have excellent interpersonal skills, and be lifelong learners, staying abreast of the most current trends, technology, and best practices in the PreK-12 educational setting.

However, this is still not enough. In the twenty-first century, school leaders must not only be able to successfully exercise all of the aforementioned leadership skills but, in doing so, also operate charismatically. This is not necessarily a new concept—that is, the benefits of leading charismatically. In fact, dating back to 1977, Robert House published a theory of charismatic leadership.

In more recent years, charismatic leadership has almost become synonymous with what we now categorize as transformational leadership, which many researchers and practitioners argue as best practice. In this type of leadership, a leader is constantly thinking of the followers' needs. The opposite of transformational leadership may very well be transactional leadership. Whereas transactional leadership "focuses on the exchanges that occur between leaders and followers" (Northouse, 2018, p. 164), transformational leadership focuses on engaging "with others and creates a connection that raises the level of motivation and morality in both the leader and the follower. This type of leader is attentive to the needs and motives of followers and tries to help followers reach their fullest potential" (Northouse, 2018, pp. 164–65). As you can see, transformational leadership would be the better approach to leading any given organization, regardless if it is a school district or school building. However, sadly, one might argue we have more transactional leaders than transformational leaders in our nation's schools.

Furthermore, one might argue that we have school leaders who do not necessarily understand the importance of leading with charisma. Thus, with *The Fourth Tier: Leadership and the Power of Charisma* by Dr. Christopher Colwell, one might further argue that we receive a desirable and timely book on exactly what it means to be a charismatic school leader in the twenty-first century. Perhaps the most important and powerful aspect of Colwell's book simply lies in the fact that he makes a strong argument that charismatic leadership can be learned.

Some earlier definitions suggest that charisma and what we have come to know as charismatic leadership is of divine origin (Weber, 1947)—that is, of, from, or like God or a god—by definition. In his latest book, Colwell leans on the most relevant, current, extant literature and research indicating that charisma can, in fact, be taught. *The Fourth Tier* reminds all of us that leadership is about relationships, namely, the relationship between leaders and followers, or in the school setting, school leaders and all stakeholders, including students, staff, parents, community members, and business owners.

Colwell iterates what matters most as it applies to school leadership (or leadership in general) by focusing on the "specific attributes of leadership that can lead to highly charismatic missions and relationships between leaders and stakeholders." In doing so, Colwell carefully articulates and reinforces the eight specific leadership skills (i.e., emotion, trust, competence, influence, energy, confidence, mission, and integrity/ethics) to ensure the success of all school leaders in the twenty-first century, who, as we know and Colwell so clearly emphasizes, operate in a highly "volatile, uncertain, complex, and ambiguous environment" on a daily basis.

There is no doubt that any school leader who can aptly combine and effectively implement the eight charismatic attributes shared within this book will most certainly be able to successfully manage the day-to-day tasks, while also serving as an instructional leader with interpersonal skills. Thus, fostering follower loyalty and further garnering support and a commitment of followers to the leader's mission, a mission that most surely aims to ensure that all students are college, career, and life ready, regardless of their demographics.

If you are a school leader in the twenty-first century, you will most certainly want to read this book, and I strongly suggest you keep it nearby for quick reference as needed.

Dr. Denver J. Fowler
Chair, School of Education
Program Chair, Doctor of Education program
Professor, PK-12 Educational Leadership
School of Education
Franklin University

Preface

Our nation's school and district leaders operate in highly volatile, uncertain, complex, and ambiguous (VUCA) environments (Bennett and Lemoine, 2014). The skills and attributes that may have produced successful education leaders in the last century may no longer be sufficient for leadership success in this modern environment of rapid change and increased societal expectations.

Success in the education sector requires highly skilled and effective school and district leaders. When those leaders are not prepared for the challenges of the modern school environment, job turnover increases, job performance and satisfaction decreases, and the ability for teachers and students to work at their optimum level is impacted.

A study by the Broad Center in 2018 found that while the average tenure for large-system superintendents was six years, superintendents working in high-poverty districts had tenures averaging three and a half years shorter than superintendents working in affluent districts. Also of concern, female superintendents had tenures that averaged fifteen months shorter than male superintendents (Superville, 2018).

A study by the Wing Institute (2019) found school principal annual turnover rates of 22 percent during the 2011–2012 academic year. The average tenure of a school principal in 2017 was just four years, with a remarkable 35 percent of school principals serving less than two years.

While many of these changes resulted as principals moved to leadership positions in other schools or took other roles in education, the impact of this high rate of annual school leadership turnover is significant. This principal turnover results in increased district costs, higher teacher turnover, and lower student achievement (Levin and Bradley, 2019).

It is clear that the greater the challenges or sense of crisis a district faces, the more rapid the turnover is for school and district leaders, creating a cascading effect that impacts every level and aspect of the education system. Leadership turnover creates stress for teachers, parents, students, and the community as a whole.

This stress results in lower student achievement as well as increased teacher turnover rates (Beteille, Kalogrides, and Loeb, 2012). This stress can lead to a lack of commitment, focus, and belief in the sanctity or viability of the school or district's mission by all stakeholders, internal and external.

Levin and Bradley (2019) found that poor preparation and weak ongoing professional development for school leaders plays a significant role in principal turnover. Conversely, the more prepared a principal is for the position, the more likely that principal is to feel successful in their work and remain on the job, even when working in high-stress environments.

The Fourth Tier: Leadership and the Power of Charisma focuses on the specific attributes of leadership that can lead to highly impactful charismatic missions and relationships between leaders and stakeholders. These charismatic leadership skills are often not taught in our universities and district leadership training programs and are often underassessed or not assessed at all by state licensing boards.

Today's education leaders must be successful and skilled at the myriad of management obligations required for teaching and learning to occur. Schools that are not well managed are schools where learning cannot occur. This first tier of leadership skill is necessary but not sufficient for success in the twenty-first century.

The second tier of leadership skill, the leader as an instructional expert, is the primary focus of most modern state and university training and licensing programs. Educational leaders are in the teaching and learning business; they certainly need to be experts in the field they lead. In VUCA environments, being a highly skilled manager and an instructional expert are not, in and of themselves, sufficient for leadership success.

Today's leaders need to develop the skills and attributes that allow all stakeholders to believe in, and rally around, powerful missions that matter. Teams on powerful missions are teams that can thrive, even in the volatile environments that surround the education sector. This focus on the mission, on what Covey (1989) calls the "big yes," defines the third tier of leadership, the mission-driven leader (Colwell, 2018).

The Fourth Tier examines eight specific leadership skills that, when combined and utilized effectively, can have a powerful impact on the overall success of the leader in meeting the challenges of education in our twenty-first-century VUCA environment. This examination places the role of charisma into context as a fourth level of leadership training that can enhance the leader's ability to be a successful manager, instructional leader, and interpersonal leader.

Perhaps at no time in our history has the role of our education system been so questioned by policy makers and yet, so important to the fundamental well-being of our society. Today's leaders in education must be equipped with the understanding and the skill set to excel in this VUCA environment.

There are specific leadership attributes that can be understood and learned concerning the nature of charisma and the role of charismatic leadership. These charismatic leadership attributes can be a key component in the professional development of twenty-first-century leaders. It is this area of leadership understanding and development, the leader as a charismatic, that defines the focus of the *Fourth Tier*.

Acknowledgments

It is a daunting task to acknowledge all of the educators, family members, and other impactful people who have made a significant impact on my career as an educator. In fact, it cannot be done. Everyone in education recognizes the countless former students, teachers, colleagues, and mentors who have shaped our careers and our work. To my colleagues throughout the education field, thank you.

To everyone who has guided me through the years, thank you for your impact and your work to make a difference in the lives of children. To my colleagues at Stetson University, thank you for your commitment to our work preparing the next generation of teachers and leaders. To the many teachers, principals, and superintendents who continue to serve as my role models, thank you.

A special thanks to Joshua Rust for your insight on the nature of the charismatic leader and to Denver Fowler for contributing the foreword to this work. To my mother, Ann Colwell, thank you for your insight into my work and support for this project.

Finally, thank you from the bottom of my heart to my wife and inspiration, Monique Colwell. Your support and guidance though all of our adventures, big and small, means the world to me.

Introduction

The Fourth Tier: Leadership and the Power of Charisma addresses an often overlooked aspect of the skills and attributes needed to be a high-performing education leader in the twenty-first century. While the literature on school leadership is extensive and highly informative for both practicing and beginning education leaders at all levels, there has been relatively little written about the important role that charismatic leadership attributes can bring to today's school and district leader.

The Fourth Tier examines the specific attributes that all charismatic leaders possess. These attributes are identifiable, are grounded in a long history of scholarly research, and can be learned. While many attributes that lead to charismatic leadership are recognized and assessed by state licensing boards, there are also significant lapses regarding certain charismatic leadership indictors and how today's leaders are trained and assessed.

The text is divided into three parts, each building on the previous section. Part I ("The Four Tiers of Education Leadership") examines four distinct leadership tiers and the attributes necessary to be successful in each tier. These tiers of leadership are all necessary but, in and of themselves, not sufficient for leadership success.

This section also examines the nature of the modern K-12 sector, which operates in volatile, uncertain, complex, and ambiguous (VUCA) environments. Finally, part I explores the components and rationale behind the need for leadership and charismatic attributes to be developed throughout the organization and not just serve as a skill set for those in position power.

Part II ("The Eight Attributes of the Charismatic Leader") defines and examines eight specific leadership attributes that all charismatic leaders possess. These attributes are explored in the context that educational leaders face. Challenges and benefits of each attribute are also examined. Where each charismatic leadership attribute is currently assessed throughout the United States as well as how current education leaders see the relative value of these charismatic attributes is also addressed. Each chapter in part II examines a specific charismatic leadership attribute with a focus on how those attributes impact the ability of the leader to thrive in today's VUCA environment.

The Fourth Tier concludes with part III ("Charismatic Leadership in Action"). This section examines the research behind the teaching and development of specific charismatic behaviors. While historically, charisma has been viewed as something magical, something that one is either born with or without, current research leads to a different conclusion. Charisma can be taught.

An examination of the power and dynamics of the charismatic follower and the symbiotic relationship between charismatic leaders and charismatic followers is also examined in part III. The interconnected nature of the eight attributes of charismatic leadership are examined. It is not any single attribute that leads to charismatic leadership but the combination of these attributes that, when combined, provide the leader with a powerful charismatic impact.

Finally, part III examines the nature of the personalized charismatic leader as a separate type and style of leadership from the socialized charismatic leaders discussed throughout this book. There are significant differences between the leadership styles and desired outcomes sought by socialized charismatics and personalized charismatics.

Part I

THE FOUR TIERS
OF EDUCATION LEADERSHIP

Chapter One

The Four Tiers of Leadership

Leadership under the best of conditions is a challenging enterprise. Leadership in the complex and volatile environments that describe today's schools is even more challenging. Gone are the days where the leader could function simply as a manager of daily operations. While management skills are required to ensure that the organization functions smoothly and efficiently, the leader who excels at management but lacks technical expertise or a mission focus will not succeed.

All highly successful leaders share certain skills and attributes. These attributes require the leader to excel in a variety of roles and in a variety of settings, each with unique organizational goals. These leadership competencies include specific personal capabilities, interpersonal skills, the ability to manage change, and the ability to focus on results (Zenger and Folkman, 2002). They all require management skills, K-12 education sector expertise, and a strong mission orientation.

Whether it is leading a technology company, a manufacturing company, or an education company, the need to have sector-specific expertise is expected, and correctly so, for today's leader. For education leaders, understanding best practices surrounding teaching and learning is a critical leadership attribute. There is a reason that all stakeholders expect the school principal, or superintendent, to be the instructional leader of the organization.

No one wants to drive an automobile designed by engineers who don't understand transportation. No one wants to go to a hospital that is run by a leader who does not understand health care systems and support structures. Certainly, no parent wants to send their child to a school led by a principal who does not understand the pedagogy of teaching and learning as well as the management skills necessary to support all the systems that support teachers and students.

A newer, third set of leadership skills focuses on the leader as an interpersonal expert with a strong focus on the mission of the organization. This mission-driven leader uses trust, team building, and powerful communication strategies to build a common mission-driven purpose for the organization as the primary leadership goal (Colwell, 2018).

Most leadership training programs, including those responsible for initial leadership licensing and those responsible for ongoing professional development for leaders already in the field, focus on the first two tiers of leadership: leadership management behavior and leadership expertise in teaching and learning. These are clearly necessary areas of focus for all leaders at any level of K-12 education.

The recognition of the importance of the leader as having strong interpersonal skills is also on the rise for many involved in the development of education leaders. This third tier of leadership skill and expertise allows the leader to form teams of educators on a common mission. With the complexity inherent in the K-12 education sector, it is critical for leadership to be distributed widely throughout the organization. This team orientation to solving complex issues requires trust and open communication between the leader and all stakeholders.

There is, however, a fourth tier of leadership skill that is not receiving enough attention from those who train and assess leaders in the field of education. This tier has as its focus the attributes of the charismatic leader. The research is clear that there are specific leadership attributes that result in a charismatic style of leadership just as there are specific leadership attributes that build leadership expertise or interpersonal skills.

These four differing leadership tiers function as a hierarchy of leadership development and effectiveness. Each tier serves as a necessary component for leadership success. Each tier builds upon the success of the leader's ability to excel in the previous tier. These four leadership tiers are the managing leader, the expert leader, the mission leader, and the charismatic leader.

TIER 1: THE MANAGING LEADER

Education today, and for that matter, education leadership today, is rooted in an organizational structure developed in the early twentieth century. This "modern" American school system is a result of the great Industrial Revolution, which had as a byproduct, the need to create an education system designed to serve large numbers of students in an efficient and effective manner. This modern American system of education for all remains remarkably unchanged nearly one hundred years later.

Just as cars and other manufactured products arose out of a mass-production system built around a highly efficient and tightly controlled bureaucratic structure, so too did the modern American education system develop as an assembly line designed to mass-produce educated students.

For much of the last one hundred years, this education assembly-line system, with each grade level serving as a station on the line, and with each station responsible for delivering very specific additions (curriculum) to the product (students), worked well. Teachers specialized in specific grade levels or subject matter and were responsible for delivering their product on time.

Education leaders were trained to be expert managers of daily operations as well as efficiency experts. The school leader served primarily as a project manager focused on safety, standardization, and efficiency (Colwell, 2018). This is the tier 1 leader, the leader as expert manager. These management experts provide a needed operational structure and accountability to the organization (Tschannen-Moran, 2009).

The managing leader is still vital to the overall health and success of today's schools. The events of recent years point out all too regularly the need for schools to be led by individuals who understand how to respond to the physical and emotional safety of students and staff alike. School and school district resources, both financial and personnel, are stretched thin, requiring leaders to be skilled at delegation and efficiency. Clearly, a well-managed education system is a prerequisite for success.

An examination of the professional development provided to aspiring school leaders, as well as current leaders in the field, will show that a great deal of time and energy is spent providing these leaders with the knowledge and skills necessary to be high-performing managers.

There are both dangers as well as significant limitations to the tier 1 leader. An examination of how many leaders spend their time will show that, for leaders at all levels of the organization hierarchy, time spent managing daily operations can be all consuming. Too many leaders find their time consumed by "firefighting," by responding to the operational challenges of the day with little time left for more strategic long-range planning.

It is not that these routing tasks are not important. That is not the danger. In fact, no classroom, school, or school district can function well if not managed well. Learning cannot take place in environments that are not physically and emotionally secure. Learning cannot take place in environments that are not well organized. No parent will leave their child in a school environment that appears to be chaotic or unsafe.

The danger for the tier 1 leader lies in believing, or getting trapped into acting as though, a well-managed school is the primary mission of the organization. It is easy to get trapped in management activity at the expense of other, equally, if not more important, leadership behaviors. For many leaders, management becomes nothing more than responding to daily events and emergencies. While a well-managed school might have been sufficient for leadership success in the past, with today's higher expectations and systems of accountability, that is certainly no longer the case.

These managing leaders develop what Everard, Morris, and Wilson (2004) call "restricted vision." The leader is blinded to any need for long-term strategic planning, team building, or mission-driven activity that rises above the routine operation of the system itself.

TIER 2: THE EXPERT LEADER

The leader as an expert in the field is certainly not a new construct. In the education sector, a variety of significant societal events over the last fifty years, coupled with increased expectations regarding the definition of success, moved leadership training and support to focus much more specifically on preparing the education leader as an instructional expert.

Safe and orderly schools run efficiently, while necessary, were not enough in an environment of international economic competition. It was recognized that school leaders must also have the expert power needed to lead high-quality teaching and learning. What is the point of having highly efficient and safe school environments if teachers are not teaching and students are not learning at the highest levels?

The space race with the Soviet Union of the 1960s, followed by the economic battles with Japan, and then with China spurred the development of the education leader as needing expertise in pedagogy. Societal satisfaction with K-12 educational outcomes was low as it appeared the Unites States was being outperformed in a variety of sectors by other countries. For effective leadership to occur in schools and school districts, leaders would be required to have instructional expertise (DuFour, 2002).

The leader as expert in the field of teaching and learning is the second tier of modern educational leadership. This notion of the instructional expert leader is now so ingrained in leadership training and evaluation that it is hard to imagine a school or district leader who is not seen as an expert in curriculum, instruction, and assessment. Today, the skilled school manager who is discovered to lack expertise in teaching and learning is doomed to failure and will not remain in a leadership position for long.

These first two tiers of leadership, the leader as high-performing manager of daily operations and the leader as instructional expert, dominate the training and professional development activities for most school leaders. Recently, however, the notion of the leader as an interpersonal expert has also emerged.

TIER 3: THE MISSION-DRIVEN LEADER

In the fast-paced world that is twenty-first-century schooling, the number of people-to-people interactions that occur on any given day is in the thousands. After all, education is a people business. Teachers are interacting constantly with other teachers, parents, support staff, administrators, and, of course, their students.

Internal and external stakeholders are also interacting with, and reacting to, the events that are occurring in the school. Shadow an educator for a day and you will see what appears to be a nonstop sequence of interpersonal interactions. The leader may be dealing with management issues, the leader may be dealing with teaching and learning issues; whatever the issue may be, however, the leader is certainly dealing with people.

It is for this reason that the skills specific to interpersonal relationships, skills such as the ability to communicate in a powerful way, to inspire and motive others, to build relationships, to collaborate with teams, and to support the development of others as leaders, are seen as so significant to the modern skill set of the high-performing leader (Zenger and Folkman, 2002).

The mission-driven leader is highly adept at interpersonal skills and is also more likely to be a successful team builder. Interpersonal skills do not require the same degree of technical expertise as pedagogical skills, and as a result the tier 3 leader is able to demonstrate attributes that can be accessed by others in the organization (Kouzes and Posner, 2010). While not every stakeholder can be an expert in the field, every stakeholder can benefit from working with leaders who are skilled at team building.

The tier 3 leader is a collaborative leader. As a result, the capacity of the leader grows as the capacity of the expanding leadership team grows (Colwell, 2018). The recognition that leadership is a team sport, that the ability of the leader to succeed is impacted by the behavior of others, is central to the development of the leader as an interpersonal expert.

It is from this commitment to the leader as having expertise in the "soft skills" of interpersonal interactions built around developing teams of leaders that the importance of the leadership team's mission arises. Tier 3 leaders are mission-building leaders. These tier 3 leadership missions all have something in common. They are missions that matter.

It is the scope and purpose of the mission that separates a tier 3 leadership activity from a tier 1 management activity. Management is important. The master schedule must run smoothly for teaching and learning to occur. The master schedule is not, however, the mission of the school; it is a condition that must be met so that the mission of the school can occur.

For the tier 3 leader, the climate and culture of the school become just as important as having a smoothly running lunchroom or testing schedule. The importance of open communication, team building, and mission focus in a culture that values the importance of the mission is a high priority for the tier 3 leader (Kelly, Thornton, and Daugherty, 2005).

The leader committed to having a profound impact on the organization recognizes the value and importance of each of these three leadership tiers. This modern leader understands the roles that management power, expert power, and mission power play in the larger picture of leadership success.

Success in each of these roles, while vitally important, does not, however, automatically result in the leader demonstrating charismatic power. This is the fourth tier of leadership, the leader as someone who has a charismatic effect on the organization.

TIER 4: THE CHARISMATIC LEADER

It is this fourth tier of leadership, the leader as a charismatic, that is the focus of this book. Like art, charisma is often seen as something that most people would describe as knowing it when they see it, but at the same time have difficulty describing the specific attributes that make someone charismatic.

In any sector it is not hard to find examples of leaders described by those in and out of the organization as charismatic figures. Media pundits will often label certain leaders as possessing charisma. There is often a "star" quality associated with the term. It is often others who connect the leader to potential followers as someone demonstrating charismatic qualities.

There is not much focus by those who identify, recruit, and train education and other leaders, however, on what the specific attributes are that make an individual charismatic in the first place. Little attention has been given regarding whether or not the attributes of charisma can be taught and enhanced in leadership behavior for individuals throughout the organization. There is a need to have a much broader understanding of how charismatic leaders can enhance the performance of schools and school districts.

What is it that separates the high-performing leader, who is skilled at all three leadership tiers but is not seen as a charismatic leader, from the leader who shares those same leadership skills as a manager, an instructional leader, and an interpersonal leader and is also recognized as possessing charismatic traits? What must occur in leadership training and selection to have leaders who are skilled at all four tiers of leadership?

In order to answer these questions, one must first understand what charisma actually is and is not. Charisma is not magic. Charisma is not something that a leader either innately possesses or is never to possess. There are specific measurable traits and attributes that are common to all charismatic leaders. The fourth tier of leadership, the charismatic leader, can be described, understood, and developed.

WHAT IS CHARISMA?

Historically, charisma has been seen as a type of divine gift, a set of skills that certain leaders possessed. Followers believed charismatic skills allowed leaders, often religious, political, or military, to accomplish impossible tasks by using the powers that had been bestowed upon them in an almost mystical way. These leaders were seen as born leaders.

The very origin of the word charisma originates from the Greek word *charis*, meaning charm (Maclachlan, 1996). Weber (1947) described the charismatic leader as an individual who is seen by followers as possessing unique qualities related to the ability to lead a group through turbulent times, through rapid and significant societal or institutional changes. In this context, charismatic leaders are much more likely to arise during times of conflict and crisis.

Arriving at a common conception and definition of charisma continues to be elusive, as many sociological and psychological theories continue to differ on their analysis of the nature of charisma and even the likelihood that the charismatic leader can ever be integrated effectively at both the operational and theoretical level (Grabo, Spisak, and van Vugt 2017). Yet there are recognized attributes that charismatic leaders possess.

There is a growing consensus that charisma results primarily from a leader possessing specific individual traits. These traits resonate deeply with followers, which begins the process of engagement between leaders and followers. Other researchers focus on the relationship between organizational and contextual factors in society at large as the primary drivers of charismatic leader and follower growth.

Grabo, Spisak, and van Vugt (2017) propose that while charismatic leaders do not rise in isolation from the myriad of contextual, physical, and social factors of any specific era, they have the ability to attract attention, arouse emotions, and articulate a vision. Stutje (2012) sees charismatic leaders as always being mission driven, articulating some type of calling.

This calling resonates with followers and offers some type of redemption or salvation for the group. This salvation requires some underlying existential threat to the group from which the leader can articulate a way out, a rescue. The charismatic leader is often seen as, or presents as, a common man of humble origins, even if the leader's background does not resemble the group background at all.

Stutje (2012) goes on to describe three preexisting conditions needed for a charismatic leader to succeed. First, there must be some type of real or imagined social crisis that is seen to threaten the group. Second, there must be some type of political space, an opening in the existing structures in which leaders and followers typically operate. These openings might manifest themselves when existing leaders are viewed as weak and ineffective, or when a new political or social force is emerging that does not yet have established leaders.

Finally, charisma, when viewed as a gift of grace from the leader, manifests itself as a quasireligious attraction between followers and the leader. As the mission being articulated becomes more and more transcendent in its scope, so too does the devotion of the follower.

Avolio and Yammarino (2013) describe the charismatic leader as someone who has a great ability to connect emotionally with followers around a common cause. Antonakis, Fenley, and Liechti (2011) define charismatic leadership as leadership that is fundamentally symbolic in nature with a strong foundation of common emotional and ideological beliefs shared between the leader and the follower.

Middleton (2005) found a direct correlation between the emergence of charismatic leaders and the emotional intelligence of the leader. Leaders who are able to monitor their own emotions as well as the emotions of others and then discriminate and use that information to guide their behaviors are demonstrating a high degree of emotional intelligence (Salovey and Mayer, 1990).

While there is a great deal of research that indicates that physical features, such as height, perceived attractiveness, even gender, play a role in the attention that certain leaders receive, it is more the charismatic leader's ability and willingness to expend an inordinate amount of energy to attract the attention of followers to the leader and the leader's cause that signals to followers that a charismatic leader is emerging.

Charismatic leaders are skilled at arousing the emotions of followers. Silvia and Beaty (2012) found that followers connect charismatic qualities to individuals who are great public speakers with strong oratorical skills—the leader as an extrovert. There are many examples of charismatic leaders whose rhetorical skills generated a strong and devoted base of followers. The stronger the emotional connection between the leader and the follower, the stronger the commitment to the leader (Shamir, House, and Arthur 1993).

These same skills are used by the charismatic leader to convey the urgency of the challenge or opportunity being faced, as well as the ability to articulate a path forward regarding what collective response is needed (Awamleh and Gardner, 1999). When coupled with the ability to generate and maintain the great deal of energy needed to attract and maintain the attention of followers in the first place as described above, it is easy to see why many see extroversion as a prerequisite for charisma.

Charismatic leaders have the ability to articulate a collective identity tied around shared values and a shared vision for a better tomorrow (Grabo, Spisak and van Vugt 2017). A leader with no followers is not a leader. Followers need much more than a leader to follow; they also need a reason to follow. What motivates people to strive for greatness, to stretch their capacity, to commit to work that is difficult, is the belief that there is a value in the mission (Colwell, 2018).

Stephen Covey describes this belief in working toward something of significance as working for the "big yes" (Covey, 1989). It is the purpose of the work that brings value to the team. Without a purpose, all work becomes routine at best and drudgery at worst. This "big yes" can, in and of itself, be a charismatic and motivating force in any organization.

Belief is a powerful motivator of human behavior and commitment. Leaders who believe strongly in a powerful mission and who are able to model that belief in word and deed are seen as charismatic, not because the leader is a great orator or extravert, but because the mission that is being articulated has meaning and power. The ability to have that sense of purpose and to communicate that purpose in a powerful and relentless way is an attribute that all high-performing leaders have in common (Zenger and Folkman, 2002).

All charismatic leaders have the ability to connect with followers around a clearly articulated vision that specifically addresses a group of people with common issues. The charismatic leader is able to connect the vision and the group through emotional, values-laden communication and demonstrate a strong sense of commitment to the group and the mission even if it means sacrifice for the leader.

The concept of the collective identity between charismatic leaders and followers is fundamental to the charismatic relationship. Charismatic leaders are able to articulate what all of the group members have in common, be that common goals or common grievances. The charismatic leader is also able to articulate a way forward, a way to reach those goals, to solve those grievances.

These groups of charismatic followers may be as large as entire nation-states, the collective identity of the country, or specific subgroups identifiable by gender, race, religion, ethnicity, socioeconomic background, geography, or experience. Often the charismatic relationship between the leader and followers begins with just a small group of highly devoted and energized individuals.

In today's social media environment, leaders have the ability to connect with large numbers of potential followers regardless of their location. The need for the speech in the town center, or even the televised speech to a larger audience, is no longer the only way to arouse strong emotions and commitments from followers. All leaders have used the tools for communicating available to them at the time.

Today's leaders have more tools and more access to groups and subgroups than ever before through many social media platforms. The louder and more far-reaching the "megaphone," the communication tools, are, the more likely it is that the audience will be larger and will not only be able to connect with the leader but with each other.

When the leader has the ability to signal to others by attracting attention, arousing emotion, and building a collective identity, the leader's ability to coordinate group action and maintain a strong sense of confidence by the group in the leader is also enhanced. With that collective action, confidence, and urgency comes a greater likelihood that the leader's objectives will be accomplished (Grabo, Spisak, and van Vugt 2017).

CHARISMATIC LIMITS

Charismatic leaders are more likely to arise, and be sustained by devoted followers, during times of great crisis or turbulence. Once that crisis or turbulence has subsided, even if it subsides as a result of the actions of the charismatic leader, the need for leaders with charismatic traits also subsides. For leaders in the education sector there is no indication that the turbulent and volatile environments in which teachers teach, students learn, and leaders lead is in anything but a steady state of crisis.

Any analysis of the education sector over the last fifty years will show an ever-increasing volatility and uncertainty. As budgets continue to be stressed and societal expectations regarding what is expected from today's schools continue to rise, the need for leaders who understand the power of specific charismatic behaviors will also continue to be in high demand by those who are currently serving in leadership positions or by those who are responsible for identifying, recruiting, retaining, and retraining school leaders at every level.

The leader as a high-performing manager or expert who can maintain the current equilibrium, while certainly possessing important leadership skills, is not equipped, based solely on those skills, to lead in times of uncertainty and crisis. This leader as manager or as instructional expert does not necessarily possess the qualities typically associated with charisma.

Charismatic leaders often come from outside the traditional corridors of power. The leader then has the ability to present as an outsider, not part of the problem but a key to the solution. Once that leader has become successful in attaining power and has begun to implement the strategies articulated to achieve the mission, it becomes much harder to present to the group as an outsider. Any future crisis or failure to deliver on the promises made can easily become connected as a failure on the part of the leader.

Leaders who are able to maintain a charismatic following over time are leaders who demonstrate a congruence between their words and their actions. For example, when leaders sacrifice their freedom for the cause (Mandela) or their life for the cause (King), follower trust and commitment to the leader's mission rises. When there is a proven disconnect between the leader's words and the leader's actions or when the leader's actions only occur in ways that exempt the leader from the consequences of those actions, follower commitment and trust falls.

Today, charismatic leaders are seen to possess certain traits and characteristics that are part of a skill set that can be developed (Grabo et al., 2017). In short, the skills that make a leader charismatic can be taught (Avolio et al., 2009). Central to the attributes that make a leader charismatic are how the leader uses eight specific skills to connect with followers in a powerful way. These charismatic attributes are:

Emotion (Antonakis et al., 2016, 2011; Avolio and Yammarino, 2013; Castelnovo et al., 2017; House, 1977; and Howell and Shamir, 2005)

Trust (Antonakis et al., 2011; Bass, 1985; Conger and Kanungo, 1988; Howell and Shamir, 2005; Keyes, 2002; Shamir et al., 1993; and Tomasello and Rakoczy, 2003)

Competence (Antonakis et al., 2011; Conger and Kanungo, 1988; and House, 1977)

Influence (Antonakis et al., 2011; Castelnovo et al., 2017; DePree, 1990; House, 1977; Shamir et al., 1993; Silvia and Beaty, 2012; and Weber, 1946)

Energy (Awamleh and Gardner, 1999; Bromley and Kirschner-Bromley, 2007; and Conger, 2015)

Confidence (Bandura, 1993; Gibson and Dembo, 1984; Goddard et al., 2000; Grabo et al., 2017; Howell and Shamir, 2005; and Katz, 2017)

Mission (Antonakis et al., 2011; Avolio and Yammarino, 2013; Covey, 1989; Grabo et al., 2017; and Popper, 2014)

Integrity/Ethics (Bromley and Kirschner-Bromley, 2007; DePree, 1990; Howell and Avolio, 1992; Ladkin and Taylor, 2010; Liebig, 1991)

How leaders in today's schools develop and use these charismatic attributes will go a long way toward determining the likelihood of leader success. Where leaders are unaware of, or uninterested in, leadership attributes such as influence, emotion, energy, and mission, the likelihood for real impact on the organization is reduced. These skills not only enhance the leader's ability to make a significant difference, they enhance follower loyalty and commitment to the leader's mission.

Chapter Two

Leading in a VUCA World

INTRODUCTION

Following the attacks of September 11, 2001, the military reexamined the nature of defending the homeland in an era where conflict between ideologies that were not connected to nation-states was occurring. Historically, the armed forces prepared for conflict against foreign governments. These governments had borders, they had armies and clearly identified infrastructures. Clearly understood objectives and goals existed on both sides of any conflict.

Conflicts against terrorist organizations, however, with no specific borders, no armies, and irrational goals, would require a different kind of leadership understanding and preparation for the military sector. The preparation for leaders in this sector that had been so effective in the past would not be sufficient to meet these new challenges.

The results of that analysis concluded that the military would need to operate successfully in what they described as a VUCA environment, that is, an environment that is volatile, uncertain, complex, and ambiguous. Changes regarding how military leaders were trained, how decision making occurred, and how the overall structure of the sector would be organized were needed in order to prepare for and succeed in this new VUCA environment.

Just as is the case with the modern military sector, today's education sector and school leaders also operate in a VUCA environment (Bennett and Lemoine, 2014). Any observer of today's education system would agree that the volatility, uncertainty, complexity, and ambiguity identified as the state of the modern world when it comes to our nation's security are also accurate descriptive words regarding the daily life of school educators and leaders.

What has worked in preparing school leaders in the past may no longer be sufficient for the twenty-first-century school leader, just as how military leaders were prepared to fight World War II may not be the most appropriate preparation for fighting the war on terrorism.

Leaders with strong management skills might be able to maintain the status quo and a sense of equilibrium when dealing with the volatility and uncertainty of the modern education environment. Management skills alone, however, will not be enough for leaders to be able to have their organizations thrive and meet significant goals without the additional skills of instructional expert, mission-driven expert, and charismatic expert.

Webster's dictionary (2019) describes volatility as a tendency for change to occur quickly and unpredictably. Today's schools are certainly subject to rapid and often unforeseen change. Education leaders at all levels of the system function on the edge of certainty on a daily basis. With so many internal and external stakeholders involved in the process, the degree of unpredictability around education issues big and small is always in place.

Education policy and regulations seem to be under constant revision from policy makers at every level of government. Policy makers who are often working under the constraints of term limits may be eager to make an impact quickly while in positions to do so. Board members are accountable to local citizens, who often expect immediate solutions to complex problems. The business community has a strong vested interest in the success of their local school system.

Teacher and leadership shortages appear to be growing as fewer young people enter the profession. The turnover of school teachers and administrators is also accelerating with the average tenure of an educator's career on the decline. All of this volatility impacts the success of the school leader and requires a specific skill set from the school leader. These are just a few examples of the impact of a volatile education environment.

Twenty-first-century school leaders must also deal effectively with all of the uncertainties that schools and school districts face. Perhaps as a byproduct of the volatility just discussed, the level of uncertainty impacting educators at all levels is also on the rise. This uncertainty appears in many forms.

For example, there is a great deal of uncertainty in the profession regarding job security. The number of states that grant tenure to teachers is on the decline. School and district leaders operate on annual contracts with no guarantee of continued employment. As budgets fluctuate, the jobs themselves held by many educators are subject to disappear from one academic year to the next.

Another significant leadership stressor involves uncertainty about the financial stability of the education sector itself. Education, with its reliance on property taxes and sales taxes, is particularly vulnerable to the rise and fall of the overall economy. That uncertainty, when coupled with policy maker budget priorities that are also in constant flux, adds to the uncertainty leaders hope for as they plan to accomplish the work.

Perhaps one of the most impactful kinds of uncertainty faced by educators is the uncertainty over whether or not the society at large actually values the work that educators are doing. When teachers and leaders do not feel that their work is valued, that the mission of educating children is seen as highly important to the culture as a whole, that uncertainty can lead to feelings of doubt about the importance of the work itself.

There is a clear connection between having a sense of value and purpose in one's work and maintaining the ability to exert the energy and commitment necessary to reach the organization's mission. Uncertainty over the perceived worth of the work itself can be devastating to the climate and culture of the school or district.

Twenty-first-century schools and school districts are also increasingly complex. The education sector is highly regulated at the local, state, and national levels. What other enterprises operate under so many jurisdictions with so many regulations? The nature of education policy development also adds to the complexity of the system as policy makers and policy philosophy both are constantly undergoing change as well.

There is, of course, some sound reasoning behind the need to ensure that our education system produces the highest possible quality of graduates. There is a direct correlation between the ability of a democracy to function and the ability for the culture to produce an informed citizenry. There is a direct correlation between the economic health of a country and the education level of the workforce.

A second area of complexity deals with the primary mission of the entire enterprise, the science of teaching and learning. It is hard to overestimate the complexity of the mission to ensure that every child in America graduates with the knowledge, skills, and values necessary to be a successful citizen. Pedagogy is multifaceted and complex. Building pedagogical systems that meet the needs of all students regardless of previous academic background is a remarkably noble, but difficult, task.

The amount of content students must master in order to be productive and competitive in the twenty-first century continues to grow exponentially. What was taught in high school in previous generations is now common curriculum for middle school students. This push downward of the curriculum continues all the way through elementary school and pre-kindergarten.

The soft skills and the technological skills needed to succeed are also on the rise. The school curriculum becomes more and more crowded while the school day and school year remain fixed with little change over the last fifty years. All these variables and expectations, including many more, add to the complex enterprise that is K-12 education.

Finally, the issues that students and their families bring to school each day are more and more complex. There is an ever-increasing expectation that school systems will be the place where society's needs are met. One reason the modern school system curriculum is so crowded is the tendency for policy makers to assign the solution of the issue to the schools.

If there is a perceived weakness in competitiveness in the world market with American mastery of science, technology, engineering, and mathematics (STEM), then policy makers add more content and assessment to those areas of the curriculum. If policy makers see a decline in civic engagement, then civics and government courses are added to the curriculum.

Any serious study of the curricular expectations over the last fifty years will show a sustained addition to the complexity of what we expect our teachers to teach and our students to learn. Yet the length of the school day and school year remains virtually unchanged over the last century.

Any one of these issues, massive regulation, highly technical and broad content and pedagogical expectations, or increasing societal expectations, would lead to a highly complex enterprise. When all three variables are in place at the same time, it is easy to see why the challenge to educate every child to the highest level is so daunting.

Finally, today's schools operate in environments that are ambiguous. This ambiguity can be seen in the variety of definitions for success that we place on the education sector. There is no agreed-upon standard for what it is the society as a whole wants all children to know upon graduation.

If one hundred citizens were selected at random and asked to define what "success" means for our schools and students, the questioner would hear a wide variety of answers. Some would say that success is rooted strictly in the academic performance of students. Others would say that success is providing each child with a sense of belonging and self-worth. Still others would argue that success is providing each child with the knowledge and values necessary to be an active, engaged citizen or is ensuring that every graduate has the skills to make a good living.

Even if there was a national consensus on the answer to this question, there is no agreed-upon standard for how the sector should assess whether or not those students can demonstrate mastery of that knowledge or skills. There is a high degree of ambiguity regarding the degree to which policy makers trust teachers and school leaders to accurately assess whether or not learning has actually occurred. Policy makers rely on standardized tests to answer the question of success, but what standardized test can accurately assess all the expected outcomes placed on today's schools?

There is also no agreed-upon standard for how teachers should be trained, evaluated, or compensated. Should teachers have tenure? Should teacher compensation be differentiated based on skill level or on supply and demand? All of these questions, and many more fundamental questions about the nature of success in K-12 education, lead to a high degree of ambiguity for stakeholders, both internal and external.

Clearly, our society has not been able to reach an agreement regarding what it means to be a successful teacher, or a successful graduate. Politically, our leaders have very different views on the purpose, scope, and function of our educational system with no clear consensus emerging. For all of these reasons, it is difficult for educators and stakeholders to see and understand what a successful education looks like. For all of these reasons, our schools operate in environments that are filled with ambiguity.

THE POWER OF CHARISMA IN VUCA ENVIRONMENTS

Weber (1947) described the charismatic leader as an individual who is seen by followers as possessing unique qualities related to the ability to lead a group through turbulent times and significant societal or institutional changes. In this modern VUCA environment, the skills and attributes that charismatic principals possess, or learn how to use, matter.

Charismatic leaders have the power to transform organizations. Charismatic leaders have the ability to mobilize stakeholders in the face of significant challenges in ways that influence the attitude and commitment of those stakeholders towards the mission of the organization (Grabo, Spisak, and van Vugt, 2017).

In very significant ways, it is the behavior of charismatic followers, however, that has the most potential for schools and school districts to accomplish significant goals. Charismatic leadership is closely correlated with increased commitment to the mission from followers in the organization as well as those without position power (Banks et al., 2017).

The charismatic leader needs interpersonal skills built on the foundation of a meaningful mission that influences stakeholders (Bligh, Pearce, and Kohles, 2006). Charismatic leaders understand the power of influence and are able to use that ability to influence large groups of stakeholders in efficient and rapid ways.

The modern education sector needs leaders adept at the attributes shared by charismatic leaders in other fields and endeavors. Charismatic leaders are having a profound impact in the automotive industry and the technology sector, to name just two examples. With focused and sustained training, charismatic leadership traits can be developed in education leaders as well.

The research of Antonakis, Fenley, and Liechti (2011) demonstrates that the attributes that leaders need to become charismatic can be developed, they can be taught. These traits impact both the leader's effectiveness and the follower's commitment to the leader and the mission. These traits yield the greatest gains in organizations undergoing rapid change. These traits align with success in VUCA environments, environments just like today's schools and school districts.

What worked for the preparation of education leaders in the last century is no more likely to be effective in this century than what worked for training military leaders in the twentieth century could be seen as sufficient training for security in our modern world. The VUCA world of today requires leaders to be highly skilled in the attributes that generate charismatic leaders and followers.

Chapter Three

The Power of Distributed Charisma

INTRODUCTION

For leaders to be successful and have significant impact in an educational environment that is volatile, uncertain, complex, and ambiguous (VUCA), it is not position power, or even expert power that matters most. It is the ability to build empowered teams on a common mission through strong interpersonal leadership skills that matters most.

The era of the leader, in any large sector, be it the military sector, the manufacturing sector, the high-tech sector, or any large enterprise for that matter, as the sole arbiter of the organization's goals, or decision-making process, is over. The world is moving too quickly for all decision making and goal setting to reside with one individual, no matter how talented or committed that individual is to the organization.

Today's leaders must be skilled at building and sustaining teams of leaders. Today's leaders must be able to distribute leadership authority throughout the organization. Today's leaders must use skills that are centered on building charismatic relationships with colleagues and building charismatic visions of the future of the organization.

THE LEADER AS EMPOWERER OF TEAMS

Like many large organizations, schools and school systems can easily begin to resemble corporate structures where all decision-making and goal-setting authority lies solely with those who hold the highest level of position power. The superintendent sets goals and delegates, with a great deal of oversight and hands-on supervision, the activities of the district staff who have been tasked to meet those goals. The district staff does the same thing to principals, principals to assistant principals, and finally task assignments are given to teachers.

Quickly, committees and teams are formed along the way to complete the work, to manage the system, to evaluate performance, and to submit reports back up the organizational line. This tightly managed framework is common in today's education sector. This top-down framework is also highly unlikely to succeed in solving complex tasks even in the best of times where the organization has ample resources.

In VUCA environments, no one individual can achieve all of the organizational goals. In VUCA environments, distributed leadership is critical. In environments with limited financial and human resources, the challenges only grow along with the need to have empowered and impactful teams in order to meet those challenges. It is always more likely that a high-performing team, rather than a highly positioned individual, will drive organizational success.

Unfortunately, highly bureaucratic organizational structures also can easily have a chilling effect on the attributes known to support a leader and the leader's mission. This chilling effect is even more problematic for organizations that can benefit from charismatic leadership teams on charismatic missions.

TEAMS AND TRUST

Trust is a critical prerequisite component for any healthy relationship to occur. Trust, or the lack thereof, between team members and leaders has a great deal to do with establishing the organization's culture and climate (Scribner et al., 2007). Cultures built upon the foundation of trust are cultures that are much more likely to achieve the goals of the organization (Gillespie and Mann, 2004).

What does it say, then, to members of the organization who do not hold positions with high degrees of job-embedded power, when those with the power of the position do not trust those individuals without position power to work on anything but routine tasks or tasks that while they may be significant to the organization are also highly managed and overseen by those in charge? Why would stakeholders commit to the mission if the stakeholder is not trusted by those in position power?

When decision-making authority is withheld from the team, so too is trust withheld. When trust is withheld, the relationship eventually dies. What gets delegated impacts trust between leaders and followers in lasting ways as well. If only routine tasks are trusted to teams, a message is being sent by leadership. That signal is not one of empowerment, trust, or confidence.

DELEGATION: CONFIDENCE AND COMPETENCE

A fundamental problem many leaders have when delegating responsibilities to others is not the need to delegate in and of itself. Effective delegation is critical for leading large and complex activities in any environment. All successful leaders delegate as a matter of survival.

The issue with leadership delegation deals directly with what gets delegated. For too many leaders, it is only the routine or mundane daily operational tasks of the organization that get delegated to others. These leaders delegate management activity believing that this then frees up the leader to focus on larger and more complex issues.

Unfortunately, this type of delegation sets up a lose-lose environment in the organization. The leader loses the opportunity to benefit from the expertise and commitment from others. The follower loses the opportunity to contribute in a meaningful way to the organization's big objectives.

For the follower, this type of delegation impacts every charismatic attribute in a negative way, including the charismatic attribute of confidence. Why should a follower, a member of the team, believe in their ability to accomplish significant organizational objectives if the boss is only delegating routine management tasks?

The act of delegation is, in and of itself, a skill set. Leaders who are highly competent at delegating recognize that what gets delegated, how it is delegated, and what happens before, during, and after the delegation occurs is important. In short, competent leaders don't delegate responsibilities to teams that do not have the expertise, the competence, to accomplish the task. Competent leaders don't delegate without also providing all the necessary resources to the team to accomplish the tasks delegated.

The leader is sending a clear message to team members by what the leader does or doesn't delegate. That message is either the leader has the confidence in the team to make critical decisions and guide the organization in a strategic way with all of the resources and authority necessary to accomplish those goals, or the message is that the leader does not have confidence in the team to accomplish objectives that are significant. As a result the team is relegated to handling only routine management tasks.

When leaders fall into the trap of delegating management activity at the exclusion of mission-driven activity, follower confidence will certainly fall. The more charismatic and impactful the mission is, the more important it is to an empowered team working on the mission.

Closely related to the attribute of confidence is the attribute of competence. Clearly, the more competent an individual is regarding any particular set of skills, the more confident that individual will be toward accomplishing the activities that skill requires. Competence, in the context of delegation, should be examined from the perspective of both the leader who is delegating as well as from the impact that delegation has on the competence of the team.

Just as with the charismatic attribute of confidence, what and how the leader is delegating also impacts the competence of the team. When followers are not provided the opportunity to learn and develop new skills, their ability, their competence in those areas, will never reach full potential. Humans learn by doing. Humans get better by practice, by failing, and by learning from those failures.

When leaders fail to provide their colleagues the opportunity to learn, practice, fail, and adapt, the overall competence of the organization falls and certainly never reaches its potential. Charismatic competence requires charismatic delegation.

DELEGATION AND ENERGY

The energy that someone puts into a task, be it large or small, is correlated with the commitment and enthusiasm the individual, or team, has for the task. Energy, commitment, motivation: these are descriptors that shed light on how a leader or a follower is reacting to the work at hand.

It is rare to see someone putting a great deal of energy into a task that is viewed as trivial or unimportant. The task might be completed, but not with enthusiasm. The task may be done on time, but with only the minimum amount of energy needed to accomplish the task.

When individuals or teams, however, view their work as fundamentally important and valuable, not only to the team, but to the larger organization as a whole, the amount of energy, both physically and mentally, that is expended on the task rises. Like many of the attributes associated with charismatic leadership, there is a symbiotic relationship between the attribute of energy and the attributes of mission, influence, and emotion.

When someone is demonstrating a great deal of energy toward a goal, they are also influencing others regarding the value and importance of the work. Why would someone be so committed to the task if it was not important? Additionally, when an individual or team commits a great deal of energy toward accomplishing something, the team develops an emotional attachment to the work.

Finally, and perhaps most importantly, there is a strong correlation between the level of energy that is committed toward any endeavor and the belief in the significance of that endeavor. In other words, the mission matters. When the mission matters, the commitment and the energy of stakeholders also rise.

If the mission that has been delegated by the leader is a basic task, the team will respond with a basic amount of energy. If the mission delegated to the team is significant, the team will commit a significant amount of energy toward accomplishing the mission. When the mission delegated to the team has charismatic qualities, the amount of energy expended to accomplish the mission will also be viewed by others as charismatic.

DELEGATION AND EMOTION

As discussed in chapter 4, emotion is one of the missing attributes for those traditionally tasked with identifying and training school leaders. State standards rarely address the attribute of emotion at all, and those few states that do assess this leadership quality see emotion and emotional impact and well-being as something that the high-performing leader should recognize in others, not in themselves (Sabina and Colwell, 2020).

These state standards do not address emotion as an attribute that can have a positive impact on the leader's ability to succeed. There is no assessment in state licensing standards that looks specifically at the relationship between the leader being emotionally invested in the work and leadership effectiveness and impact on others.

The same lack of significance on the attribute of emotion was found in a study conducted by Sabina and Colwell (2020) that asked school leaders at every level of the organization to rank the importance of charismatic leadership attributes. The attribute of emotion consistently ranked as one of the least important leadership attributes.

The research is clear, however, that when leaders invest emotionally in their work, commitment to that work in other colleagues rises. The same is true regarding what and how leaders delegate. Teams asked to complete routine work, while often necessary for the overall success of the organization, will simply not invest emotionally in that work to the degree that that same team will invest emotionally in work that matters to the team as something of worth, of significance.

DELEGATION AND INFLUENCE

While each charismatic attribute is impacted in either a positive or negative way based on how leaders delegate to their teams, the attributes of influence and mission may be the most consequential. The ability for members of any team to be influential, that is to make a difference in how the organization is functioning as well as how others in the organization are thinking about the organization—is tied to the role the team has been assigned.

The assignment given to the team not only says a great deal about the degree of influence that members of the team may have, it also says a great deal about the degree of influence the leader actually has. How leaders delegate, and what leaders delegate, impacts the ability of everyone involved in the process to be influential.

When leaders don't trust colleagues up or down the organization's hierarchy with significant mission-driven assignments, they are also limiting their colleagues' ability to influence up and down the organization. When the leader limits delegated responsibilities to routine tasks, the leader is limiting leadership influence. When the leader only wants to share the routine daily operations of the system, the leader by default is only exerting influence on those same limited topics. The same influence-killing effect occurs for those delegated routine assignments only.

For the team to influence others in a significant way, the team needs significant work. The team needs to work on missions that matter. It is possible, however, for the team, or individual members of the team, to attempt to exert a greater amount of influence on the organization as a whole by moving beyond the boundaries and scope of the team's assignments.

One can even see that teams that deliberately move beyond their assigned scope are demonstrating charismatic attributes such as confidence, competence, emotion, and energy. The team in this case is deliberately moving beyond the constructs of the delegated work. The team is attempting to influence the organization by attempting to do what leadership in this case is not doing: delegate work that matters and provides more meaning to the team as well as the overall organization.

While this can, and often does, work, it is important to recognize the leadership failure that has occurred. When leaders delegate in ways that constrain the ability of others to influence the organization, the leader is forcing the team to make choices that, with more sophisticated approaches to delegation, would not be necessary.

The team can choose to work only on the tasks delegated as those were the tasks assigned. This approach satisfies the role assigned to the team but does not satisfy the team's potential to make a difference on a larger scale. As a result, the team will not be able to generate charismatic behaviors because the mission assigned to the team yields little or no charismatic effect. As a result, great organizational potential is lost.

The team can instead choose to independently move beyond the delegated scope of the assignment as described earlier. While the potential for charismatic impact may now occur, there is also more potential for organizational conflict. The leader may respond by not assigning any work of real meaning in the future or even disband the team in an attempt to limit the power of those attempting to move beyond their assigned responsibilities.

The leader may also respond defensively and feel that their position power is being openly challenged when teams or individuals appear to move beyond their assigned scope of work. The leader may react by moving even further away from delegating work that is influential to others.

The solution to this quandary is relatively straightforward. Leaders who wish to have greater influence need to be leaders who delegate influential missions. Leaders who recognize the value of having other influential members of the organization need to delegate missions that matter to the team.

DELEGATION AND MISSION

When thinking about all of the attributes that make up the charismatic leader, and when recognizing the clear interdependence these standards have, it is perhaps the attribute of mission that serves as the centerpiece of leader delegation that has the most charismatic impact on the team. Charismatic missions, which by their very nature are aspirational missions, missions that are so challenging that many would see them as unattainable, provide the energy and the emotional connection to the work.

Delegated missions that are charismatic make it much more likely that leaders will be able to influence others in support of the mission. When employees, wherever they are in the organization hierarchy, feel connected to charismatic missions, their willingness to become experts regarding the mission increases. Team members will advocate for the mission with much greater energy and commitment (Leithwood and Jantzi, 2000).

This commitment to the mission will often also result in greater competence of the team as a whole as individuals on the team work to learn the knowledge and skills necessary to accomplish the mission. As competence rises, so too does confidence.

When it comes to delegation, it is the mission that has been delegated that matters most. Even the most well-managed and organized systems of leader-follower delegation won't have significant impact if the delegated mission itself isn't impactful.

THE LEADER AS A CHARISMATIC TEAM MEMBER

Leaders wishing to empower teams with charismatic attributes do not delegate work to the team; they join the team. It is important, however, that the position power leader is not seen as in charge of the team. It must be clear that the leader trusts the team and empowers the team to function as equals regardless of their team member's formal position power within the organization.

The charismatic leader is not working from the perspective of the organizational structure as a top-down hierarchy but from the view that the structure is a circle in which leadership is distributed and shared collectively by an empowered team (Colwell, 2018; Pearce et al., 2010).

When leaders begin by trusting the team, particularly those with less position power, the leader is demonstrating not only a level of respect for, and confidence in, the employees who work for them, they are demonstrating a commitment to distributed authority and responsibility to the team.

THE CHARISMATIC TEAM

What motivates followers to act on behalf of the leader and whether the team perceives the relationship with the leader to be subordinate to the leader or a partner with the leader, has a fundamental impact on the ability of the leader to be successful (Haslam, Reicher, and Platow, 2010).

Imagine individuals working well down the organization's hierarchy who possess charismatic attributes such as energy, emotion, confidence, and influence. Now imagine those same people in teams, who are not in formal leadership roles, but who are united around a common organizational mission. People who possess the attributes that lead to charismatic behaviors can be widely distributed throughout the organization.

This is one reason why, so often, charismatic leaders rise from the ranks or from positions of relative obscurity. Position power is not a prerequisite for the charismatic leader. If individuals can possess or develop charismatic attributes from anywhere in the organization, so can teams of individuals when given the right parameters and support for their work.

None of these team-building and team-empowering structures can occur without the leader possessing the attributes of the charismatic: *Influence, Energy, Emotion, Competence, Confidence, Trust, Mission*, and *Ethics*. The leader must also recognize, however, that the team itself has the same capacity to develop the attributes of charisma.

The leader who recognizes that the attributes of charisma are widely distributed throughout the organization is empowering the team with the potential to have a charismatic impact on the organization as a whole. This leadership behavior has the effect of trust and commitment being returned back to the leader by those with less position power (Colwell, 2018; Conger, Kanungo, and Menon, 2000). In short, by distributing charismatic potential to the team members, the leader is enhancing their own charismatic effect on others.

Sabina and Colwell (2020) studied the attributes that followers found most impactful on their ability to be successful, regardless of their position in the organization. Remarkably, the attributes that made a follower impactful aligned with the attributes that made a leader successful. In any role, the charismatic behaviors that make a difference for leaders also make a difference for followers. Just as individuals can assume charismatic status in any system, so too can teams of individuals assume that same status.

Perhaps one of the most significant examples of a charismatic team would be the legendary musical group, the Beatles. While it is evident that any one member of the group possessed charismatic attributes, it is more accurate to say that it was the group itself, the sum of the parts, that actually possessed charisma.

The Beatles were, and still are to this day, a charismatic brand. It is the Beatles' brand itself that demonstrates the attributes of charisma. The group itself has not existed for almost fifty years. Two of the four members of the group have died, and yet the charismatic nature of the Beatles did not stop with the passing of the individual members of the team or with the passing of time.

Perhaps the most significant aspect of a charismatic team versus a charismatic individual is the potential for the team, made up of multiple members, to continue their charismatic work despite the individual makeup of the team. When a charismatic figure retires or passes away, the charismatic mission may cease as well, unless there is a charismatic team or a charismatic organization in place to carry on.

What is most impactful, however, is not the rise of a charismatic leader or even the charismatic team, it is the development of the charismatic organization.

THE CHARISMATIC ORGANIZATION

While the literature regarding the attributes and impact of charismatic individuals is extensive, there has not been a similar focus on the concept of charismatic teams, as discussed earlier, or on the concept of the charismatic organization. If teams of people can acquire charismatic attributes, so too can entire organizations.

Charismatic organizations have great potential for success in a variety of areas that organizations that have not developed a charismatic focus and a charismatic following simply do not have. These advantages include strategic planning, succession planning, and stability—even in times of crisis or uncertainty.

When the institution itself is demonstrating charismatic qualities, the ability to develop and succeed at long-term strategic planning is greatly enhanced. Think of the great charismatic figures of our time. Individuals like Martin Luther King Jr. or Steve Jobs spent their lives with a singular focus and passion toward their mission.

In fact, when these charismatic leaders died, many wondered if their dream had also died. Look at the media response to the death of Steve Jobs in 2011 and the amount of press speculating on whether Apple, as a leader in next-generation technologies, could continue to thrive. An entire generation wondered whether Martin Luther King Jr.'s dream of a just society had also ended with his assassination.

In both of these cases, however, there were individuals, teams, and organizations ready, willing, and fully committed to carrying on the charismatic leaders' missions. When the organization's culture, the brand, has the same mission, energy, emotion, competence, confidence, ability to influence, and trust that the leader has demonstrated, the organization itself has the capacity to function in the same charismatic fashion as the leader.

This carrying on of the leader's charisma and charismatic mission allows the organization to plan effectively across long periods of time. The ability to weather short-term setbacks or unanticipated obstacles is greatly enhanced when the attributes of charisma are widely distributed throughout the organization. Many organizations are trapped into short-term planning and are thus unable to sustain themselves over time, particularly when faced with VUCA environments.

History is replete with examples of thriving institutions who vanished quickly due to their inability to foresee and adapt to rapidly changing environments. In fact, the ability to adapt to rapid change is a prerequisite for long-term organizational success. This ability to adapt to change or handle crisis is much more likely to occur in charismatic organizations.

How then does an organization develop the attributes of charisma? As with the development of charismatic teams, how the leader sees his or her role in the organization is critical. When the leader, in word and deed, demonstrates to both internal and external stakeholders that the leader is a member of the organization, not just in charge of the organization, the potential for the transfer of charisma from the individual to the institution is possible.

When the leader is functioning as the individual in charge, as the person through which all major decisions occur, the likelihood that the institution itself can acquire charisma is greatly limited. It is the socialized charismatic leader, the leader who is driven by an external mission, who is most likely to recognize that distributed charisma has the greatest potential for mission success.

When that recognition of the power of distributed leadership is coupled with a strategic effort to empower colleagues throughout the system with the attributes of charisma, the beginnings of a charismatic organization can begin to take hold.

As mentioned earlier, charismatic institutions are also more likely to sustain themselves over time than organizations that rely on isolated leaders with centralized power. When institutions are not firmly grounded with a unique identity, purpose, sense of values, and strategic mission, leadership changes can easily result in large swings in organizational identity and purpose.

Think of schools where anxiety is high due to a change in the principalship. Why does that anxiety exist? It is because the members of the institution itself are not confident that the new leader will adhere to the institution's norms of governance and mission identity.

When the school is relatively calm about leadership transitions, it is because the school recognizes that the institution itself is greater than any one individual. The team recognizes that for the new leader to be successful, the leader will need to adapt to the culture and norms that already exist. The more powerful that sense of institution identity and mission is, that sense of the institution as a charismatic brand, the smoother that leadership succession will be.

The notion of distributing leadership authority is certainly not something new. The consideration of how leadership manifests itself in charismatic fashions and how that charismatic identity itself can be distributed to empowered teams or to the organization itself, however, is not commonly considered by those developing and supporting educational leaders.

In the next chapters, a thorough review of these charismatic leadership attributes will be examined. These standards can be learned by stakeholders and can enhance the probability of mission success and organizational purpose.

Part II

THE EIGHT ATTRIBUTES OF THE CHARISMATIC LEADER

Chapter Four

Emotion

The Missing Standard

INTRODUCTION

As discussed in chapter 1, there are many levels (what this author calls tiers) of leadership responsibility, each requiring a specific set of leadership skills and focus. These tiers are: tier 1, management power; tier 2, expert power; tier 3, mission power; and tier 4, charismatic power.

Each of these leadership tiers focuses on specific aspects of educational leadership. The attributes that are needed to be a high-performing manager (tier 1), for example, are not necessarily the same attributes needed to be a successful leader with expert power (tier 2) or a mission-focused leader (tier 3).

Certain leadership attributes play a more foundational role in leadership success than others when looking at the specific leadership role in question. Of course, core attributes, such as the ability to lead from a position of integrity or to lead in a confident and competent manner, cross all levels of leadership.

While not a foundational skill for tier 1 management leadership or tier 2 expert leadership, for the tier 4 charismatic leader, the attribute of emotion is critical for success. The power of emotion and symbolism can be a tool that distinct communities use to organize themselves, to label their ideologies, and to communicate around a common language (Cohen, 2015).

Charismatic leaders recognize the power of emotion and are able to present the leader's primary mission in symbolic ways that resonate with followers. The symbol becomes a connection to something that the leader and the follower already know and value, which is the mission itself.

Symbols, and the emotional connections that are made, can be extremely potent. These symbols can attain almost mythlike status, resulting in great potency for the charismatic leader. The tier 1 managing leader will typically focus on efficiency and accountability, and the tier 2 leader will focus on knowledge and expertise around pedagogy. The tier 3 leader focuses on the primary mission of the organization. The tier 4 charismatic leader, however, also has a focus on the emotional connections between stakeholders and between those stakeholders and the mission itself.

The use of emotion and symbolism takes the relationship between leaders and followers past a rational relationship based solely on leadership authority or the use of information to guide decisions or interactions (Turner, 2014). The power of the relationship itself between the charismatic leader and the charismatic follower is strong. When it is grounded in an emotional connection, the strength and commitment to that relationship between leader and follower only grows.

Tier 3 leaders are focused on the primary mission of the organization and are driven to deliver the mission successfully. These leaders are typically goal oriented. These leaders recognize that good management is necessary to accomplish the mission but not sufficient. They use expert power and many of the same attributes that tier 4 charismatic leaders use. Like the tier 4 charismatic leader, the successful tier 3 leader has integrity, energy, competence, and a strong ability to influence.

When that tier 3 leader is able to articulate a new mission for the organization, a mission that to many would seem impossible yet resonates with followers, the leader is beginning to demonstrate tier 4 charismatic qualities. When the mission is charismatic, it is by definition connected symbolically and/or emotionally to both the leader and the follower.

The charismatic leader and the charismatic follower care deeply about the mission. The mission resonates on more than a rational or intellectual level; it resonates as a symbol, as a dream of what can be. That dream is rooted in emotion and symbolism.

CHARISMA, BELIEF, AND THE POWER OF EMOTION

Leaders must combine many attributes to make a charismatic connection with followers. Clearly the charismatic leader has the competence, confidence, and energy to promote their cause. All of that energy and confidence, however, must be combined with the ability to use symbolism and emotion to connect with followers in more than just a rationale, intellectual way. Charismatic leaders must also have the ability to arouse the emotions of followers.

The stronger the emotional connection between the leader and the follower, the stronger the commitment to the leader (Shamir, Houser, and Arthur 1993). It is one thing to intellectually agree with the position a leader takes. It is another to believe in that position or that leader to the degree that the follower will exert great energy and commit resources over an extended period of time to the leader and the leader's cause.

Avolio and Yammarino (2013) describe the charismatic leader as someone who has a great ability to connect emotionally with followers around a common cause. Antonakis, Fenley, and Liechti (2011) see charismatic leaders using a leadership style that is fundamentally symbolic in nature with a strong foundation of common emotional and ideological beliefs shared between the leader and the follower.

In a study involving charisma and beginning leaders, Middleton (2005) found a direct correlation between the emergence of charismatic leaders and the emotional intelligence of the leader. Leaders who are able to monitor their own emotions as well as the emotions of others and then discriminate and use that information to guide their behaviors are demonstrating a high degree of emotional intelligence (Salovey and Mayer, 1990).

Belief is a powerful motivator. Leaders who hold and, more importantly, demonstrate strong beliefs and the followers who share those beliefs see in the leader someone who is truly committed to a significant cause. This belief brings more energy, more commitment, and more purpose to the work of both the leader and the follower.

For the charismatic leader, the beliefs that are espoused are rooted more in an emotional context than in an intellectual context. Military leaders, for example, use emotion and symbolism to connect righteous and patriotic causes to the battles at hand. Their soldiers can connect emotionally to the causes for which they are fighting.

If soldiers feel the symbolism and the emotional connection to a cause that represents something bigger than themselves, they can demonstrate a kind of charismatic, larger-than-life ability to do what would in other contexts never occur.

A belief in the significance of the undertaking becomes such a powerful, emotional, motivating force that soldiers will literally risk their lives based on the power of their belief, their sense of duty, and their unwavering commitment to support their brothers and sisters in arms.

When we think of charismatic figures throughout history, this use of symbolism and emotion to motivate and inspire others is a common attribute that links all charismatic figures together. Missions that are routine are just tasks to be checked off a "to do" list. Missions that are larger than life are a totally different enterprise, however, with totally different kinds of relationships between the leader and the follower.

Think of President Kennedy and the language and symbolism he used to announce his goal of having the United States send a man to moon and back in the 1960s. Think of Martin Luther King Jr.'s famous "I Have a Dream" speech on the Washington, D.C., mall in front of 100,000 people calling for racial and social justice. Their call is rooted in imagery and symbolism. Their call attempts to connect with their listeners in an emotional way.

BELIEVING IN THE ASPIRATIONAL MISSION

Both Kennedy and King used the power of emotion to connect with large groups of followers around large and audacious tasks. The relationship between the significance of the task espoused by charismatic leaders and the emotional connection to the task is critically important.

There was no rational reason at the time to believe that either King's or Kennedy's mission could be accomplished. At the time of Kennedy's speech, the American space program was seen as a failure when compared to the accomplishments of the Soviet Union. US rockets were blowing up on the launchpad.

There was no infrastructure in place to accomplish a mission to the moon when Kennedy articulated his charismatic mission. There was no certainty of success. In fact, fundamental technologies that would be needed to accomplish the task did not even exist. Kennedy's call to send a man to the moon and back was, in a very real way, an impossible dream. His call was for his followers to believe in the dream anyway.

When King spoke on the steps of the Lincoln Memorial, racial injustice was, in many ways, codified in law across the United States. Decades of racial injustice enforced by law enforcement and the criminal justice system were the norm. Racial minorities were not represented politically and were often denied the right to vote. Countless liberties and freedoms guaranteed to white citizens did not exist for people of color.

In spite of these institutional barriers, King called for a complete transformation of the American culture through nonviolent protest. His speeches are wonderful examples of the use of imagery, symbolism, spirituality, and emotion to connect with followers. King had rationality and justice on his side. He needed, however, to connect with his listeners on a deeper emotional level, and he did just that.

In many ways, the examples of King and Kennedy, who were both great orators, help spread the idea that to be charismatic, one must be an extrovert and a great public speaker. That is not necessarily the case. While many charismatic figures are also great speakers and writers, many are able to use emotion and symbolism connected to powerful missions without great oratorical prowess.

Senator Bernie Sanders created a charismatic relationship with his followers during the 2016 presidential election. Young people flocked to his campaign. Large numbers came to campaign events. An examination of his appearance and speaking style, however, does not align with the typical image of the charismatic figure. Sanders is not young, is not a great orator, and does not present himself in finely tailored attire.

The same could be said for another clearly charismatic figure, Mother Teresa. No one equates Mother Teresa to her great speeches; she didn't give any. She had no publicity machine, no rallies, and no budget. All of these leaders had something in common, however. These leaders all articulated powerful missions and used emotion and symbolism to help get their message across.

It was the scope of these missions, along with the power of the belief in the righteousness of the missions described by charismatic leaders such as Kennedy and King, that made them charismatic in the first place. It is the power of the emotional connection to the big mission, what Covey (1989) describes as the "big yes" clearly held by these leaders, which others found, and still find today, so inspiring.

Small, routine tasks do not inspire. Missions that are centered on managing organizations, or on making organizations more efficient, or even on solving organizational issues, while necessary, are not, in and of themselves, motiving or inspiring to others. There is no such thing as a charismatic manager. There is no such thing as a routine task that is also seen by others as a charismatic task. There is no emotional connection between leaders and followers to the routine or the mundane.

It is the big, bold, impossible dream that provides a charismatic aura to an individual. For a charismatic relationship to occur between leaders and followers, the mission itself must be bigger than life, the mission must, from a purely logical, intellectual perspective, appear to be impossible. As Kennedy said, "We do these things not because they are easy, but because they are hard" (Kennedy, 1962).

EMOTION: DRIVING ENERGY
FOR THE CHARISMATIC MISSION

It is the scope of the dream itself that requires the leader to connect on an emotional level with others. The bigger the mission, the more important it becomes to build a symbolic, emotional connection to the mission itself. Emotion in many ways is a prerequisite for energy. The definition of the word itself derives from the Latin word *emotere*, meaning energy in motion.

It is the emotional connection that fuels the energy that allows the leader and the follower to stay focused on the dream. Commitment is connected to how one feels. The stronger the feeling toward the worthiness of the cause or the work, the stronger the commitment toward that cause or work becomes (Askins, 2009).

Emotions generate energy. Charismatic leaders understand the relationship between emotions and energy and how to harness the energy of emotions toward the leader's mission. It is emotion that provides the energy that drives the movement of the organization (Cooper and Sawaf, 1998). That energy increases when the leader is able to use the power of symbolism, of metaphors, to connect with and capture the follower's attention.

EMOTIONAL INTELLIGENCE

There is a significant aspect of leadership that is commonly referred to as emotional intelligence (EI) (Mayer, Salovey, and Sluyter, 1997). Caruso and Salovey (2004) have identified four leadership skills tied directly to the understanding of, and use of, emotional intelligence for leaders.

These four EI skills involve the leader's ability to (1) perceive emotion, (2) use emotion to facilitate thought, (3) understand emotions, and (4) manage emotions. All of these components can be measured. All of these components can be taught. And yet, in most leadership licensing systems, not a great deal of attention is paid to this important component of leadership.

While most educational leadership assessment systems do recognize the value of the leader being able to perceive the emotions of others, there is very little attention paid in the state processes used to assess leader readiness around the ability to use emotion to facilitate thinking, understand emotions and the information those emotions convey, or manage emotions to promote the organization's goals (Sabina and Colwell, 2020).

Caruso and Salovey (2004) argue that like many other leadership attributes connected to charisma, the attribute of emotion can be developed and improved over time. Charismatic leaders are able to use emotional information to guide their actions and decision-making processes. There are emotional skills that leaders need just as there are analytical skills that leaders need. Like all skill sets, with practice and understanding, those skills can be enhanced.

It is the combination of high performance in leadership skills that integrate rational and analytical thought and decision making with the effective use of emotional leadership styles that leads to high-performing leaders (Caruso and Salovey, 2004).

How people feel impacts the quality of their work and their commitment to the work. When teams of people begin to experience the same emotions or have their emotions begin to feed off of each other and reinforce each other, a kind of "emotional contagion" takes place. Charismatic leaders understand the powerful impact that this contagion can have on the group and the groups' commitment to the leader and the leader's mission.

Caruso and Salovey's (2004) work on the nature of, and power of, emotional intelligence for leadership success identifies six principles of EI that charismatic leaders understand and master. Those leadership principles are:

1. Emotion is information; information about people.

   All effective leaders understand the power of information. Education, in particular, has become a data-driven enterprise. Schools have data "war rooms," conduct "data chats" with their faculty, and establish data-driven goals. Too often, however, the information that is being gathered does not include emotional data. Emotional data can be just as valuable to the leader as any other form of data.

2. Emotion can be ignored, but that will not work.

   There is a cost to ignoring, or not understanding, the role that emotion plays in the leader's and the organization's success. Just because the leader is not emotionally intelligent does not mean that the emotions of the leader and the emotions of the followers are not influencing organizational effectiveness, employee judgment, and employee energy and commitment to the work.

3. Leaders can try to hide emotion but will not succeed in doing so.

   The idea of the leader as always calm and steady no matter how turbulent or uncertain the organization's situation may be is deeply rooted in leadership training culture. This notion that emotions should be suppressed and that the show of emotion is counter to successful leadership is a process referred to as normalizing emotion (Ashforth and Kreiner, 2002).

   While leaders may be trained to hide their feelings, these attempts to suppress emotion almost always fail. Every colleague, every stakeholder, will see the leader's body language, tone of voice, displays of emotion, even if temporary, at some point or another. Emotionally intelligent colleagues and stakeholders will see it all of the time (Caruso and Salovey, 2004).

4. Effective decisions incorporate the emotional component.

   Leaders are taught to be rational. Of course, we need reasoned thought and intellect; we need our leaders to have expert power. We need to see this reasoned and rational behavior evident, and in use, by our leaders. In fact, a feeling that the leader does not have emotional self-control or the ability to empathize with the emotions of others would be seen as a fatal leadership flaw.

What is often missing, however, in the training of future leaders, or the evaluation of current leaders, is the understanding that human emotions are part of every decision-making process and that the failure to recognize the important role that emotions play in leadership and decision making is, in and of itself, a form of irrationality. If we want leaders to be rational, then we need leaders who understand the powerful role that emotions play in leadership and followership.

5. Emotions follow a logical pattern.

Like any scientific inquiry, the emotional behavior of humans can be seen to follow specific patterns and sequences. Emotional behavior can be quantified, understood, and often predicted. Emotions can be mapped (Plutchik, 1994) and leveraged for the good of the organization and the leader. This ability to leverage the power of, and predictability of, emotional response is a critical attribute of the charismatic leader.

6. There are emotional universals just as there are specifics.

As Caruso and Salovey (2004) point out, a smile is recognized as a smile in every culture, just as emotional displays of fear, anxiety, or contentment tend to be universal in nature. What varies from culture to culture are the social circumstances in which emotional displays are considered appropriate. Understanding the cultural norms of emotions are critical for the high-performing leader and certainly for the charismatic leader.

It is important to be reminded that this entire sector of leadership development, the leader as a powerful user of emotion, appears to be the least identified and understood leadership attribute in the field of leadership training and assessment. This is the case despite the research-based evidence that connects the power of emotion to the success of the leader. Emotion, while critical for a charismatic form of leadership to emerge, is often the missing standard in leadership training and assessment.

EMOTION: THE MISSING STANDARD

In a study conducted by Sabina and Colwell (2020) of all fifty state licensing standards along with the District of Columbia, the authors found that while half of the states in the country address the attribute of emotion in some context, the majority of those states only refer to the ability of the leader to understand the emotional state of others and not the role of emotion in the leaders themselves as a charismatic leadership indicator or an attribute that will increase the leadership effectiveness of the leader.

While half of the states in the country make no mention of the role that emotion should play in leadership, for the twenty-five states that do reference a connection between emotion and leadership, sixteen of those states do so only in the context of having the leader work to ensure that the social-emotional needs of others are met.

For the states assessing leadership and emotion, the goal of the leader regarding the attribute of emotion is to ensure and support the emotional well-being of students and staff, not to recognize the role that emotion plays in the performance and effectiveness of the leaders themselves. These states attempt to assess the leader's ability to recognize the emotional well-being of followers and stakeholders and to attend to those issues as they arise in an appropriate and effective manner.

Only nine states have leadership standards that call for leaders to lead with "emotional insight" (Arizona, Arkansas, Delaware, Idaho, Maryland, New Jersey, New York, North Carolina, and Vermont); or call on the leader to be self-reflective regarding their own emotional intelligence in order to "manage oneself through self-awareness and self-management . . . to manage relationships through empathy, social awareness and relationship management. This competency is critical to building strong, transparent, trusting relationships throughout the school community" (North Carolina).

The failure of many licensing and regulatory agencies responsible for determining the criteria for high-performing school leaders to recognize the role that emotion, that passion and commitment, play in the leader-follower dynamic is an area of concern. An emotional commitment to the mission is not only a prerequisite for all leaders striving to have a charismatic impact on others, it is also a prerequisite for mission success.

It is hard for leaders or followers to exert great amounts of energy for a cause in which there is no emotional attachment. It is hard to be mission driven if you are not emotionally connected to the mission itself. It is hard to take the time to learn, to develop expert power, on a mission that is viewed as routine.

VOICES FROM THE FIELD

As mentioned earlier, the leadership attribute of emotion is largely missing from the state standards used in the United States to assess and license educational leaders. Where the attribute of emotion is measured, it is limited to assessing the degree to which the school leader is aware of, and sensitive to, the emotional needs of others.

A study by Sabina and Colwell (2020) of 130 educational leaders across Central Florida, and their ranking of the importance of charismatic leadership attributes to leadership success, found the attribute of emotion to also be underappreciated.

Regardless of the level of the leader, from school superintendent to first-year assistant principal, emotion as a high-impact attribute for leadership success consistently ranked at or near the bottom of charismatic leadership attributes. When those who serve primarily in positions as influential followers of leaders were asked the same question, the results were the same. Followers did not place a high value on emotion as an important contributor to their success.

And yet, despite the absence of states assessing the power of, and effective use of, emotion in leadership behavior or the perceived lack of the importance of emotion as an attribute for the Sabina and Colwell (2020) sample, it is a common sentiment from educators at every level that students don't care how much the teacher knows until they know how much the teacher cares.

The same is true regarding the importance of the relationship between leaders and followers. Followers also don't care how much the leader knows if they don't believe that the leader cares. In this case it is an understanding from the follower that the leader not only cares about each follower, each colleague in the organization, but also that the leader cares about the mission.

This notion that relationships precede learning, that relationships are an integral part of the teacher learner process, is not new or contested. It is also true that most relationships have more meaning and more significance when the relationship includes some common emotional bond or connection. There is a connection between the quality of the social relationship and the emotional connections between those in the relationship (Ryff and Singer, 2001).

When leaders show high levels of trust in others, they are demonstrating confidence in, and regard for, those with less authority. When leaders show that they care, they are demonstrating an emotional connection to each individual on the team. For the charismatic leader, the team is not just a collection of nameless, interchangeable workers in the system; the team is made up of real people with lives that matter to the leader.

It is the emotional connection that the leader demonstrates by word and deed that assigns a charismatic quality to all involved, both leaders and followers. An emotional connection to the team is necessary but not sufficient for charismatic leadership to emerge. The charismatic leader also demonstrates an emotional connection to the mission itself. Just as everyone in the organization wants to be valued and connected with as an individual of worth, so too does everyone want to be connected with missions that matter.

If the leader has no passion for the big goals of the organization, why should anyone else have passion for the work? If the leader doesn't seem to care about whether or not the organization meets its goals, no one else is likely to care. How then does the leader demonstrate caring for the mission? It is the emotional connection to the value of the mission that first indicates to followers that a charismatic leader is emerging.

THE EMOTIONAL CHARISMATIC

As will be discussed in later chapters, one unique aspect of the charismatic leader is the need for the leader to be able to demonstrate all of the attributes necessary for charisma. In short, having any one charismatic attribute does not result in a charismatic leader-follower relationship. Charismatic leadership requires expertise in all attributes connected to charisma. Perhaps this is one of the reasons there are so few leaders who are typically described by others as charismatic leaders.

A leader who is skilled in the understanding and use of emotion as a tool for mission success and stakeholder buy-in is not necessarily a leader who is seen by others as charismatic. In short, for the charismatic leader to emerge, the attribute of emotion is necessary but not sufficient. Emotional connections to the mission and the team must be connected with the attributes of trust, competence, integrity, confidence, and, most importantly, an aspirational mission.

Clearly, the charismatic leader is a leader who connects on a symbolic and emotional level with stakeholders. The charismatic is not only emotionally connected to the team, to the followers, but, more importantly, to the mission itself.

Chapter Five

Building Systemic Trust

INTRODUCTION

Trust matters. As anyone studying effective leadership traits, serving as a leader, or reporting to a leader knows, when relationships are built upon a framework of trust, the overall effectiveness of the organization, and the ability for meaningful collaboration to occur, rises. Trust impacts every aspect of the organization's culture and climate (Harris, 2003; Scribner et al., 2007).

Tschannen-Moran (2014) identifies trust as the bond that inspires others to reach higher levels of achievement and exert greater effort toward the leader's mission. From this point of view, trust becomes a prerequisite for individuals and teams to reach their potential. Trust, or the lack thereof, becomes a key performance indicator regarding the overall health of the organization's culture and the ability of the organization to reach lofty goals.

When teams of people, large or small, are dependent on each other for success, the need for trust between the members of the unit is critical. All leaders and followers have an interdependent relationship to some degree. No leader can succeed in isolation, no team can function without leadership. As a result, trust is an attribute that works both ways; leaders must trust in the follower and followers trust in the leader.

Zenger and Folkman (2002) have identified key leadership competencies covering specific leadership categories such as character, personal capabilities, focusing on results, interpersonal skills, and leading change. While each of the competencies needed for success in these categories matter and are required for highly effective leadership to occur, it is the category of interpersonal skill development that stands out as a key factor for successful high-impact leadership.

The ability to build powerful and positive relationships, to inspire and motive others, to communicate in powerful ways, and to collaborate with a team of people define the competencies of a leader highly skilled in interpersonal relationships. A critical component of all of these interpersonal skill competencies is trust. It is trust, respect, and belief in a powerful mission that unite leaders and followers around what Covey refers to as a belief in the "big yes" (Covey, 1989).

These attributes are increasingly necessary in the complex world of twenty-first-century schools, where the responsibilities and job roles for school principals has grown exponentially (Rousmaniere, 2013). The more followers trust their leaders, the more committed they become to following the leader's words and deeds (Stutje, 2012).

Zenger and Folkman (2019) identify relationships, expertise, and consistency as the elements most necessary for trust to occur. It makes sense that there is a strong correlation between the degree to which someone feels they have a positive relationship with another individual and the degree to which that individual feels they are in a trusting relationship. Relationships precede trust. Relationships matter most.

When individuals know that they can count on someone to do what they say they are going to do and demonstrate consistency in word and deed over time, trust is also more likely to occur and be maintained. Inconsistency leads to doubt and anxiety. Doubt and anxiety kill confidence and trust.

Finally, trust rises as individual confidence in the expertise of the leader rises. For one to trust in the mission that the leader espouses, one must also trust that the leader has the expert power to accomplish the mission. No one is going to trust a leader they view as lacking the fundamental competence to accomplish their role.

The attribute of trust is also found in leaders who are viewed by followers as charismatic. Scholars studying the attributes possessed by all charismatic leaders find that trust plays a pivotal role in both how the leader interacts with followers and how followers interact with leaders (Antonakis, Fenley, and Liechti, 2011; Howell and Shamir, 2005).

All healthy relationships require some degree of trust. For a relationship to take on a charismatic quality between leaders and followers, however, the necessity of the attribute of trust as a prerequisite for charismatic power to occur cannot be overstated.

Since charisma is directly connected to leaders who display larger-than-life attributes of energy, emotion, and confidence, or who advocate for larger-than-life missions, the ability for large groups of people to trust that the charismatic persona is real, or that the mission is attainable, is critical. Charismatic followers must trust that the leader has the competence, as well as the other attributes of charismatic leadership, necessary to accomplish the goal.

Simply put, the charismatic follower must trust the charismatic leader. The charismatic leader must also trust the charismatic follower. While the nature and orientation of how that trust manifests itself varies between followers of socialized charismatic leaders and personalized charismatic leaders (to be discussed further in upcoming chapters), the attribute of trust remains a critical prerequisite for all charismatic relationships.

THE THREE ORIENTATIONS OF TRUST

Trusting Up

For most leaders and followers, not much attention is given to the orientation of trust. Should followers begin each day trusting their leaders? Should leaders begin each day trusting their followers? Who should trust who first is not often discussed. All relationships do, however, have a base orientation, an expectation, regarding trust and how leaders in the larger organization behave and expect others to behave.

Many leaders may argue that trust doesn't begin anywhere but is earned over time as individuals prove themselves to be trustworthy. For these individuals, trust is something that emerges over time, often based on the experiences any one individual has had with any other individual. The notion that one must earn trust is common throughout our culture. Trust does, however, typically have an orientation, a place where trust begins.

Most leaders expect the relationship between leaders and followers to begin with the follower recognizing that the leader has been placed into a position of authority for a reason. The leader has expert power and position power because others, even higher up the organization, have trust that the leader is the right person for the job.

If those who hire leaders have trust in the leader's ability and character, shouldn't those much further down the organization's hierarchy also begin their relationship with the leader by placing their trust in the leader to do the right thing? For most leaders and organizations, the answer to this question is yes. This is a trusting-up orientation.

Most hierarchical organization have this orientation. The follower is expected to begin the relationship by trusting-up to the leader. The leader has more expertise, more authority, and greater access to information. It is assumed that the leader is to be trusted by the follower to be making the best decisions for the organization as a whole and for the individuals with less position power in the organization.

The formal structure for establishing trust is built upon an expectation that those at the lower rungs of the organizational structure will trust-up to the leaders who reside at the top of the pyramid, where all of the position power lives. The organization operates on an assumption that those who are not leaders in the hierarchy begin each day, each activity, trusting those who lead them (Colwell, 2018).

High-performing leaders will recognize that the trust that they expect to receive from followers can easily be lost if the leader does not follow through on promises made, but the leader still begins by assuming that the relationship starts with the subordinate trusting-up to the leader to do the right thing.

Trusting Down

As discussed earlier, trust is a prerequisite for employee motivation and commitment to the task (Leithwood and Jantzi, 2000). Particularly when the mission at hand has charismatic attributes—that is, the mission itself is bold, audacious, and difficult—trust must exist between leaders and followers.

When leaders begin relationships with colleagues and stakeholders by trusting those individuals instead of expecting those colleagues and stakeholders to begin by trusting them, the leader is demonstrating a trusting-down orientation. The leaders who are trusting-down are showing confidence in their colleagues' ability to do their jobs well.

The trusting-down leader is not working from the perspective of the organizational structure as a pyramid where those with position power can expect trust based on their position in the organization, but from the view that the organizational structure is flat, a structure in which leadership is distributed and shared collectively by an empowered team (Pearce et al., 2011).

When leaders begin by trusting-down to those with less position power, they are demonstrating a level of confidence in the employees who work for them. Leaders who demonstrate trust that the team can help in significant ways to accomplish the mission are more likely to earn high levels of trust and commitment from the team and to the mission of the leader in return (Conger, Kanungo, and Menon, 2000).

When someone is working on a team for a leader who appears to trust them, the individual will begin to feel more empowered and autonomous. Perhaps most importantly, the individual will begin to develop a larger sense of competence and confidence that they can accomplish the mission (Spreitzer, 1995).

This positive byproduct of a trusting-down orientation is particularly important when looking at charismatic missions, which by their very nature are significant, challenging, and often seen as unattainable by most people. When followers are trusted with important information or important tasks to complete, the confidence, energy, and mission-driven focus of those followers will increase. In short, this orientation toward trust has the effect of dispersing charismatic attributes that the leader possesses to the follower as well.

Trusting down increases collaboration and commitment to the work by followers. Trusting down increases the capacity of the team and makes it more likely that the team will expand in both membership and influence. Trusting down increases the autonomy of followers to act independently in their work to accomplish the mission (Colwell, 2018).

Finally, for a socialized charismatic relationship to occur, it is trust between the leader and followers that the mission comes first, that it is the value and righteousness of the mission that binds everyone, the leader and the follower, together. This is the next orientation for trust. This is trust in the mission itself.

Trusting the Mission

What unites followers and leaders in a socialized charismatic relationship is a common belief in, and passion for, a big idea that resonates with the team as a whole. In a way it is the mission, not the relationships between people, that bonds the team in a trusting way. Put simply, the socialized charismatic relationship is a charismatic mission-driven relationship as much as it is a person-to-person relationship, as discussed further in chapter 10.

Socialized charismatic leaders demonstrate overwhelming trust and faith in the power of the mission itself. Socialized charismatic followers do the same thing; they trust the value and importance of the mission above all else.

Since it is the power of the mission that matters most, it becomes extremely important for the followers of charismatic leaders to trust that the leader is fully committed to the mission. Charismatic follower trust will waiver if the leader's commitment to their charismatic mission appears to waiver.

It is equally important that the leader trusts that the mission is also the primary driving and uniting force for all followers. Socialized charismatic leaders need to trust that their followers share the same values and commitment regarding the worth of the primary mission that binds the group together in the first place.

In this context, both the leader and the follower are subservient to the mission itself. There is truly a team orientation around this common bond of the big, audacious mission. The charismatic leader must trust that the followers will stay fully committed to the mission. If followers, for any reason, choose to abandon the mission, they are simultaneously abandoning the leader.

The inverse is also true. Followers of charismatic missions must trust that the leader will remain true to the mission. Should the leader abandon the mission, the follower sees the leader as abandoning them. It is the deeply held trust that followers and leaders believe in the sanctity of the mission that binds the leader and followers together.

Competence and confidence are also necessary attributes for charismatic leaders. It is sometimes not reasonable to assume that a charismatic mission can be accomplished. Charismatic leaders, however, demonstrate confidence in the value of the mission and the attainability of a mission other leaders would describe as folly.

When followers trust that, despite the odds or uncertainty, the charismatic leader does have the competence and the confidence to achieve the mission, trust rises. When that charismatic trust in the value and possibility of mission success is sustained over time by the leader, follower commitment to the leader and the mission also rises and is sustained through difficult times.

In a similar way, when the leader sees the confidence and competence of their followers rising over time, the leader's confidence that those followers can be trusted to stay the course rises as well. Like all aspects of a healthy and strong relationship, the component of trust is a two-way street. Leaders need to trust their followers every bit as much as followers need to trust their leaders.

Trust inspires a sense of worthiness of belonging to the group and the group's mission, and as a result the individual becomes more and more willing to cooperate with and support the mission of the leader (Rhoades and Eisenberger, 2002). This is what empowered teams look like.

TRUST OTHERS TO HAVE THE BIG IDEA

For the charismatic leader, the origin of the idea is not as important as the idea itself. In a sense, it is the mission itself that gets all of the credit and provides all of the value to the leader and the follower. The socialized charismatic leader is just one of many powerful and effective voices for the mission. The charismatic mission belongs to everyone, not just the leader.

The socialized charismatic follower is also not interested in who thought of the mission first or who gets credit for the idea. What is critically important to the charismatic follower is the trust that is built and maintained around fidelity to the mission between the leader and the follower. What is important to the follower is the leader's ability to articulate the mission and demonstrate that they can be trusted and that the leader possesses all of the charismatic attributes discussed in this book to carry out the mission successfully.

The socialized charismatic follower sees the leader as subservient to the mission itself: The value of the mission is foremost. The follower trusts in the commitment of the leader to stay true to that mission. Trust in the capacity of the leader to stay true to the mission and to accomplish the mission is vital.

VOICES FROM THE FIELD

Sabina and Colwell's (2020) analysis of how the leadership attribute of trust is incorporated into the licensing and assessing for all education leaders found that trust is measured by just over half of the states in the country. Trust ranks as the third most assessed leadership trait by state licensing agencies behind the charismatic attributes of mission, assessed by forty-nine states, and the attribute of integrity/ethics, assessed by forty-six states.

Thirty-two of the fifty states assess the degree to which leaders are able to demonstrate trust and understand the role that trust plays in successful leadership. These states recognize the important role that trust plays in developing positive working relationships, providing open lines of communication, and nurturing a culture of collaboration and high expectations.

While trust ranks higher than leadership attributes such as competence, influence, and confidence, it is startling to see that eighteen states are silent regarding the role that trust plays in successful education leadership. While other charismatic attributes, such as energy and emotion, might be predicted to be rarely taught and assessed due to the fundamental nature of trust as a prerequisite for leadership success, it is unsettling to see so many states not explicitly addressing this leadership attribute.

As with the other charismatic attributes studied by Sabina and Colwell (2020), there is no correlation between the geographic region of the state and whether the attribute of trust is assessed or the size of the state and the attribute's presence in the licensing process. States in every region of the country are assessing trust and states in every region of the country are not assessing trust. There are examples of states with small populations as well as large populations assessing trust and vice versa.

An examination of leaders serving in the field, however, found the attribute of trust to be highly correlated with leadership success (Sabina and Colwell, 2020). Only the attribute of integrity/ethics was viewed as more important than the attribute of trust by the practicing leaders who were surveyed.

Regardless of the leader's position in the system, from high-ranking district leaders to beginning assistant principals, trust was seen as a vital prerequisite for leadership success. When those who see their primary function in the organization as that of a follower, the same high ranking of the importance of trust was found. Both leaders and followers ranked the charismatic attribute of integrity/ethics first and the attribute of trust second.

THE TRUSTING CHARISMATIC

Charismatic leaders are trusted leaders. Socialized charismatics, both leaders and followers, are also charismatic mission-driven individuals and teams. The trust that is built between charismatic leaders and followers centers around a certainty that it is the mission above all else that matters.

An example of this type of charismatic trust in the sanctity of the mission above all else can be found in Elon Musk, the founder of Tesla and SpaceX. Musk is widely recognized as a charismatic figure. He has a dedicated charismatic following including more than twenty-four million followers on Twitter.

Like many charismatic leaders, he has both a devoted following and harsh critics. Like most charismatics, he is a disrupter of the status quo. Musk is an example of the leader who possesses all of the attributes of charisma: emotion, trust, competence, influence, energy, mission, and integrity.

While Musk certainly wants his companies to succeed, grow, and be profitable (his work ethic and long hours at his factories are legendary), he consistently demonstrates in word and deed a higher mission, a charismatic mission. That mission is to transform the world's transportation systems away from an oil-based economy to a more sustainable, ecofriendly economy.

Examples of this charismatic trust in the mission can be seen with Musk's sharing on the internet all his patents for his electric automobiles (Korosec, 2014). Clearly, an executive whose primary mission is profit, or the success of his company at the expense of other competitors, would never share trade secrets.

This behavior only makes sense if one is to believe that there is one thing even more important to Musk than the success of his company. That one thing is the transformation of the economy away from carbon-based energy. That is the charismatic mission. That is the mission that Musk's millions of followers are attracted to.

Perhaps the clearest example of the charismatic leader trusting the value of the mission above all else can be found in a 2018 interview with Musk on the television series *60 Minutes* (Stahl, 2018). In that interview, Musk is asked if his car company failed but the world automotive industry successfully transitioned to electric cars, would he be happy and consider himself successful.

His answer is a charismatic one. His answer demonstrates the connection between charisma, mission, and trust. His answer is yes. The mission itself, the automobile industry transitioning away from oil to electricity, is more important than the success of the company he started to achieve that goal.

Musk's followers also believe in that mission but, as importantly, also believe that Musk believes in the mission and is willing to sacrifice everything in order to accomplish the mission. As a result, Musk's charismatic followers are also willing to sacrifice. The follower buys the Musk dream, so the follower buys the Musk car, even if they could buy another car at a much cheaper cost. This is the trusting charismatic in action.

Chapter Six

Competence

The Prerequisite Standard

COMPETENCE DEFINED

Regardless of the profession, or even any specific task to be accomplished, no one wants to work with, be led by, or have a service provided by someone who is incompetent. In fact, a basic lack of competence is typically clear grounds for termination in most professions, including education. A look at any state's professional code of conduct will show that a failure to demonstrate consistently a competent level of performance will be grounds for dismissal.

Webster's dictionary defines competence as "having requisite or adequate ability or qualities." This definition clearly connects competence to adequacy. A competent individual is up to the task. They have the necessary skills to meet at least the minimum performance standards of the task or job at hand. Competence is also often thought of in terms of expert power and a set of intellectual skills and expertise in one's chosen field.

In every profession, once a lack of competence is established, the individual will either lose their job or their customers. Competence in the field of leadership is no different than any other profession. The competent leader has a fundamental ability to meet the leadership tasks at hand.

The competent leader has the necessary prerequisite leadership attributes and expert power necessary to meet the job requirements of that position. The licensing of educational leaders by state departments of education is, in fact, a fundamental exercise and assessment designed to ensure leadership competence.

Competence is not only a prerequisite for licensing, it is also a prerequisite for follower confidence. The more competent that stakeholders perceive the leader to be, the more committed those followers become to the leader's message and style (Castelnovo, Popper, and Koren 2017).

Stakeholders' views on leadership effectiveness as well as the follower's commitment to the leader are tied directly to the perceptions of the leader's ability to demonstrate high levels of competence (Antonakis, Fenley, and Liechti, 2011). As leader competence rises, leadership ability to influence and build trust between leaders and followers also rises.

IT'S THE DOING THAT IS HARD

Look at any organization, any team of people, large or small, and you will find the vast majority of those individuals ready to speak up when it comes to identifying a problem in the organization. It is also not hard to find colleagues who have plenty of opinions regarding how to solve any particular issue. It is not rare or unusual for meetings to become overwhelmed by so many voices identifying problem areas and what needs to be done to solve those same problems.

It is the doing that gets hard, however. When it comes time to actually decide on, and implement, the recommended solutions, the number of colleagues who are ready to step up to the plate will often suddenly diminish in number. In too many organizations or teams, everyone has their ideas regarding what should be done but few really commit the time and energy needed to actually implement those recommended solutions.

There are many factors that might account for the difference between the number of people willing to help identify issues, or suggest solutions to those issues, and the number of people willing to actually do the work necessary to make those solutions a reality. For some it may simply be a matter of time management or prioritizing what is most important to that individual. These individuals have the competence to achieve the necessary changes, but they simply don't have the time or the interest to do so.

For other members of the team or the organization, the ability, the competence, to successfully carry out the task may be the limiting factor. These individuals do not lead change because they lack the skills or the confidence to do so.

It is the getting things done, however, that actually leads to organizational change. The best plans in the world, the best intentions in the world, do not result in anything at all if not put into effect. Leaders who are competent are more likely to be change agents, to follow through, to build empowered and skilled teams and actually do something. It is in this context that competence and charisma connect; the competence to make meaningful and difficult change a reality is a charismatic leadership prerequisite.

COMPETENCE: THE SURPRISING CHARISMATIC ATTRIBUTE

When one thinks about charismatic figures that have been encountered over time, the attribute of competence is not what leaps to mind. Ask anyone to describe what a charismatic person looks or acts like, and you will hear words like inspiring, extroverted, smart, or visionary.

Martin Luther King Jr.'s "I Have a Dream" speech will never be described as an example of competent public speaking. John F. Kennedy's speech announcing the goal of sending a man to the moon will never be described as an adequate example of a technological quest. When asked to describe a charismatic figure, it is highly unlikely that one will hear competency as a charismatic descriptor.

In fact, for many, the term competency is a kind of faint praise. It is easy to imagine hearing someone described as a competent individual as having the implied meaning that the individual has average ability, can certainly get the job done, but there is really nothing special about that person.

When praising and recognizing excellence in someone, competence is not the attribute that will be highlighted. No one attends a retirement ceremony or hears a funeral elegy where the person being honored is described as being a competent person. Why then is competence one of the eight attributes necessary for charismatic leadership?

When examining the role of competence in the development and success of the socialized charismatic, however, a very specific dynamic emerges. Because the socialized charismatic tends to focus on the importance of the mission itself, so too are those who are attracted to the leader as a socialized charismatic individual. It is the power and importance of the mission that matters most to both the leader and the follower (see chapter 10 for a full discussion on the attribute of mission and charisma).

If the leader is not able to demonstrate a high degree of competence in the skills needed to accomplish the mission, follower confidence will begin to disappear. Once that confidence that followers have in the leader is gone, so too is the leader's charismatic power.

While followers of personalized charismatics will remain loyal to the personalized charismatic leader (see chapter 15), followers of socialized mission-driven charismatic leaders will abandon the leader when a lack of competence is displayed. Why would someone who is highly committed to achieving a certain goal follow a leader who does not demonstrate the ability to achieve that goal?

Like other specific attributes associated with charismatic leadership, competence, in and of itself, is not sufficient for charismatic relationships to emerge between leaders and followers. Competence is, however, a necessary prerequisite attribute for the socialized charismatic leader.

There are many examples in this modern age of technological innovation of socialized charismatic leaders who displayed remarkable levels of competence in their field. People such as Steve Jobs with Apple and Elon Musk with Tesla are viewed as charismatic transformational leaders. Their success in leading transformational changes within their respective industries is built upon the foundation of competence.

Like all socialized charismatic individuals, these men clearly demonstrated all of the attributes of the charismatic leader. Competence, even expertise or genius levels of expert power is not enough for charisma to emerge. These individuals also connected with others on an emotional level. They used symbolism and the power of big ideas to energize others.

It is the ability to demonstrate success, however, to deliver on the mission, to deliver the product that legitimizes the leader. If Jobs or Musk had not been able to do that, the charismatic aspect of their leadership would have diminished or failed altogether.

For the socialized charismatic leader and follower, the mission must be bold and transformational. The mission must also, however, be viewed as achievable or, better yet, demonstrated to be achievable. It is the underlying competence of the leader that allows that mission success to occur.

COMPETENCE AND VOICES FROM THE FIELD

While competence in one's profession is often taken for granted as a prerequisite for position success, less than half of the state licensing agencies for education leadership directly assess the attribute of competence as a leadership skill (Sabina and Colwell, 2020). Only the charismatic attributes of influence (assessed by twenty-one states), energy, (assessed by five states), and confidence (assessed by zero states) receive less attention from state boards of education than the attribute of competence.

Sabina and Colwell (2020) also surveyed more than one hundred leaders in the field of education to assess how those leaders, from all grade levels and position titles, ranked the relative importance of fifteen leadership traits commonly recognized in the literature as important attributes for success. Included in those fifteen traits were those attributes connected explicitly with socialized charismatic leaders.

Unlike state boards, who placed a relatively low value on the attribute of leadership competence as an assessed trait for licensure, the leaders surveyed ranked competence as the fifth most important attribute out of the fifteen attributes assessed. Only the leadership attributes of ethics/integrity, trust, mission, and communication ranked higher than competence.

Along with the standard of competence, three of the five highest-rated leadership attributes were also attributes connected to charismatic leadership. Of the top five standards identified by those practicing school and district leaders (ethics/integrity, trust, mission, communication, and competence), only the standard of communication is not considered a charismatic leadership attribute.

It is interesting to note that these leaders rated competence as a more impactful leadership standard than decision making, collaboration, and focusing on results, all of which are much more commonly identified in the literature, or in state assessment systems, as of critical importance as comparted to the attribute of leadership competence.

Chapter Seven

Influence across the Tiers

INFLUENCE DEFINED

Webster's Dictionary defines "influence" as "the power or capacity of causing an effect in indirect or intangible ways." To influence someone is not to order someone. Influence requires something more than just authority or position power. There is a clear difference between ordering or directing someone to do something and influencing someone to do the same thing.

As such, influence can arise from anywhere within the organizational hierarchy. While leaders in powerful positions can certainly exert influence, there is no explicit correlation between having position power and having the ability to influence others. Anyone who has worked with teams in organizations large and small has witnessed the ability of colleagues with little or no position authority to exert significant influence on the decision making and attitudes of the larger group.

While leaders can be influential at any time, and any activity may have an influence on others, too often leaders rely on the power of the position as the primary method for getting things done. These leaders may believe that they are influencing stakeholders toward a particular point of view or activity.

In fact, if influence is the ability to cause an effect on others without direct command, then no behavior based solely on position power is actually influential. Only compliance results from behaviors directed from superiors. By definition, one cannot command another person to be "influenced" by decree.

Like many other attributes for successful leadership, the attribute of influence can also exist at every leadership tier. Leaders who function primarily as managers (tier 1) are just as capable of high degrees of influence as leaders who function primarily as expert leaders. Tier 2 instructional experts can use the power of that expertise to influence others. Tier 3 mission leaders can use the importance of the mission itself to influence and motivate others.

Pink (2012) has identified the ability to influence as a critically important leadership attribute. What differentiates the ability to influence is not so much what the leader is spending time on but on how the leader exercises the use of expert power, mission power, and, hopefully, charismatic power.

While the leader as an expert (tier 2) is something most leaders aspire to and recognize as a form of legitimate influence, often that expertise is never really there or subsides over time as the leader's commitment to lifelong learning fades or is simply overwhelmed by daily tier 1 management responsibilities.

Other leaders develop and maintain expert power but fail to recognize the importance of identifying, defining, and sharing powerful missions with stakeholders. The power of the mission (tier 3) as an influencer is lost. Finally, fewer still understand and commit to developing the attributes necessary to influence in a way that results in charismatic (tier 4) leader-follower relationships.

INFLUENCE AND POSITION POWER

Traditionally, leadership has been highly correlated with position power. By default, our leaders were those in positions of power. The higher the leader's position resided in the organizational structure, the more leadership authority and responsibility was conferred. This default to the leader as the individual in charge certainly still exists today. There are both historic and practical reasons for this correlation between the leader and the position held.

The power of each position does come with specific levels of authority that are unique to that job title. The higher that position resides in the organizational hierarchy, the more power is conferred to the holder of that position. Not everyone has the authority to hire or fire or evaluate. Not everyone has the authority to set organization-wide goals or establish budgets. Position power is real and legally articulated in contracts and job descriptions.

There is also a concurrent deference to those who hold position power that is typically given to the position leader by those who hold lower-level jobs. Often subordinates will yield additional power to those in positions of authority that are actually beyond what the position contractually provides. Sometimes this deference and awarding of additional authority occurs because those who report to the position leader are unaware of the position power limits held by their supervisor.

Other times, these subordinates do not want the responsibility of decision making that actually resides within their authority and defer that authority to the position leader because it is easier. Perhaps these stakeholders don't want to be held responsible for the decision outcome. All of this results in a kind of power deference that provides even more authority to the position leader than is there.

For many decades and for most sectors, including education, the military, and manufacturing, this model of power residing with those in positions of authority and accepted without question by those who report to those position leaders has been the dominant leadership model.

Today, however, across all sectors, the decline of position power is evident. Top-down leadership that relies on position power, while necessary for certain managerial functions and organizational accountability, is no longer sufficient for organizational success. In VUCA environments, the likelihood of organizational success in highly bureaucratic top-down leadership models is even less likely.

The examples of leadership failure where the leader fails due to an over-reliance on position power are numerous and cross all sectors. The power of the position may be intoxicating, and those who behave in an authoritarian fashion may succeed in the short run, but damage to the organization's reputation and effectiveness will eventually occur.

The education sector is no different. The age of the superintendent or principal as unquestioned leader based simply on the job title is long gone. The same is true for the position of classroom teacher. Parents, and even students, no longer defer to the classroom teacher's judgments or behaviors simply because the teacher is "in charge" of the classroom.

Any cursory review of social media will show countless examples of subordinates at all levels of the organization publicly questioning or attacking the authority and judgment of leaders holding position power.

On any day, google "controversial topics in education" and see the countless examples of position power under attack. Examples of teachers organizing and striking to regain curriculum and assessment authority, teacher preparation programs under attack, and parent concerns about homework, grading policies, and the overreliance on standardized tests are just a few of the topics that appear. In each case those bringing concerns and attempting to influence the system are not operating from positions of authority or position power.

As mentioned earlier, being influenced by someone and complying with someone are not the same. Leaders who rely on position power to influence the behavior of others often see simple compliance. While follower compliance may seem like a satisfactory result for the leader, those employees who behave in certain ways not as a result of the leader's influence but only for the purpose of remaining in compliance with leadership directives are not likely to maintain that behavior to comply once the leader or the leader's power is gone.

Position power is the weakest form of leadership power. The resulting "influence" that position power gives is the weakest form of influence. As position power weakens, so too does the degree to which followers simply comply with the leader's directives. It should be every leader's goal to limit the use of position power to responding to issues associated with safety and with ethical breaches of conduct (Colwell, 2018). For all other leadership goals, the use of expert power, mission power, and charismatic power are far more likely to result in long-term organizational success.

INFLUENCE AND EXPERT POWER

Position power is obviously limited to those who hold those powerful positions. While it is certainly true that those in positions of power may also possess expert power, it is not a certainty that the two types of power (position and expert) are always present.

It is typically assumed by those who select individuals for positions of authority, as well as those members of the organization who report to authority figures, that those individuals do indeed possess real expertise in the areas they lead. Most interview and selection processes attempt to ascertain the level of expertise of the applicant.

Those who select leaders will look at education, experience, and evidence of success in similar positions as evidence that the individual has the expertise to fill the position. Interviews and reference checks will attempt to confirm that the individual has the necessary expertise to accomplish the job.

It is also true that by the very nature of hierarchical organizations, certainly including P-12 education systems, the number of leaders who actually hold position power is very small when compared to the total number of employees in the organization. A typical elementary school may have fifty employees and only two administrators. A large comprehensive high school may have up to two hundred employees and as few as five or six administrators with position power.

Expert power, on the other hand, can be, and often is, much more widely distributed. There are no real organizational constraints to the number of employees who can acquire and yield expert power and the influence that that expertise brings with it. Expert power is not a byproduct of position title. Expert power cannot be controlled as a resource to be handed down by those in positions of authority. In fact, many high-performing leaders recognize that one of the keys to leadership success is to grow the leadership capacity of others by increasing the expertise of others.

As a result, expert power has much more potential to influence the organization on a large scale than position power. This influence grows as the number of employees, regardless of their position or rank within the overall organization, grows. If the smartest person in the room is the room, then the way to increase expertise is to make the room bigger. If the smartest person in the room is the room, then the way to increase expertise is to build the capacity for those in the room to learn more.

Leaders who use expert power are much more likely to actually influence the behavior of followers in a meaningful way than leaders who rely solely on position power. Expertise does not automatically come with any position title. Expertise is earned. Expertise is a descriptor that others attribute to a leader; it is not something that can be simply declared by the leader.

When followers do believe that the leader has great competence, great expertise, the follower is more likely to also feel confident in, and influenced by, that expert power. As long as the leader continues to demonstrate expertise, the leader has influence, even if the leader ceases to function, or has never officially functioned, in some leadership capacity.

INFLUENCE AND MISSION POWER

When expert power is combined with mission power, the ability to influence others in profound ways is maximized. The need for work that is intrinsically meaningful is a critical component for worker contentment (Aziri, 2011). Employee compliance from position power becomes employee influence from expert power and ultimately becomes employee passion from mission power. The highest levels of energy and emotional commitment to the work occur when the work itself has meaning to the individual.

Mission-driven leaders understand that there is pride and purpose in all work. That purpose, however, must be clearly identified and described to those doing the work. That purpose must be shared, or better yet, that purpose must be mutually developed, so those doing the work have a say in how the work is done and improved upon.

Mission-driven leaders recognize the power of meaningful empowerment and work hard to celebrate the contributions of everyone involved in accomplishing any mission. The larger and more significant the mission is to the overall success of the organization, the more impactful mission influence can become.

The ability for leaders to identify missions that matter and to have the expertise to see how those missions can be successfully accomplished by empowering teams results in the ability to influence in significant and lasting ways. It is this combination of expertise and mission power that marks the beginnings of charismatic influence.

INFLUENCE AND CHARISMATIC POWER

Rousmaniere (2013) identified influence as one of the key leadership attributes necessary for success in the complex world of modern school leadership. As the complexity of the organization rises, so too does the need for the leader to be able to exert a great deal of influence across the organization. The more volatile, uncertain, complex, and ambiguous an organization is, the more powerful the impact of charismatic influence.

Charismatic leaders have the ability to attract attention, arouse emotions, and articulate a vision; in short, to exert a great deal of influence on others. Stutje (2012) sees charismatic leaders as always being mission driven, articulating some type of calling that has a profound influence on those who come into contact with the leader.

Charismatic leaders who can influence the direction of the organization and those who make up the organization are, by their nature, transformational leaders. Burns (1978) identifies the transformational leader as a leader with a profound vision for the future that is clearly articulated and highly impactful to followers. That profound vision is the charismatic mission.

Charismatic leaders are also great communicators. It is not enough to have a compelling vision and a strong desire to achieve that vision. Charismatic leaders transform the organization by their actions, their energy, their vision, and their ability to communicate to followers in ways that enhance the followers' belief that the vision can be accomplished.

At its essence, this is the ability of the leader to influence followers, one of the fundamental dimensions of charismatic leadership (Bass and Avolio, 1989). Influence increases when the leader has optimism, energy, clear vision, and a framework for accomplishing their vision.

When the charismatic leader combines a clear vision with creativity, communication, passion, energy, ethics, and trust in followers, and then acts in ways that empower followers to act on the leader's vision, organizational transformation can occur (Bromley and Kirschner-Bromley, 2007). All of these attributes for transformational leadership are attributes shared by charismatic leaders.

The charismatic leader can emerge from anywhere within the organization. Just as position power is not a prerequisite for the ability to influence others, position power is also not a prerequisite for charismatic leadership. In fact, in many cases, the charismatic leader emerges from within the rank-and-file members of the organization. None of the attributes that make someone charismatic require position power.

In fact, the charismatic power of influence often rises, and is viewed with more respect and impact, when the influencer is someone from humble origins or who possesses no power other than the power of their ideas.

Nelson Mandela's influence as a charismatic leader increased as he served an unjust prison sentence in South Africa. Martin Luther King Jr. had no position power, was often jailed, and relied on the power of his mission to influence others.

Gandhi was arrested multiple times during his work to secure India's independence from Great Britain. His use of passive resistance and his extreme ascetic lifestyle proved highly influential and charismatic. None of these charismatic leaders had or used position power to influence others.

Certainly, one of the more enduring and controversial aspects of modern American life can be found in the struggle over the Second Amendment right to bear arms versus the right to live in safety and free from mass shootings. While individuals with great position power on both sides of this debate fail to reach mutually agreeable solutions, those with some of the least position power in our society, school students, are demonstrating the power of charismatic influence on this topic.

A prime example of influence without power comes from the students of Stoneman Douglas High School and their impact on the debate regarding mass shootings. On February 14, 2018, a mass murderer killed seventeen students, teachers, and school staff. While regrettably not the first, or the last, of these mass-casualty events in schools, the influence of students speaking out was impactful.

National media outlets began to cover and report extensively on the work of this group of student survivors. Multiple national rallies attracted tens of thousands of participants and large social media campaigns emerged and proved successful at influencing corporate sponsorships of certain media outlets, all from the work of a relatively small group of mission-driven teenagers.

It is clear that charismatic influence can have profound impacts on organizational success as well as individual commitment to accomplishing organizational goals. A focus on the power of influence as a key attribute of leadership success remains surprisingly elusive, however.

VOICES FROM THE FIELD

The Sabina and Colwell (2020) study found that only twenty-one states assess the ability of educational leaders to influence others as part of state licensing criteria. Only the charismatic attributes of energy and confidence were assessed by fewer states (see table 7.1).

Table 7.1.   US State Rankings of Socialized Charismatic Standards for Licensure

Socialized Charismatic Attribute	Attribute Ranking
Mission/Vision	1
Integrity/Ethics	2
Trust	3
Emotion	4
Competence	5
Influence	6
Energy	7
Confidence	8

State licensing agencies are not the only stakeholders who place a relatively low value on the importance of influence as a leadership attribute. A survey of 150 leaders from across multiple school districts in Florida found that school and district leaders at all levels consistently ranked the attribute of influence in the middle of impactful leadership attributes (Sabina and Colwell, 2020).

Of the fifteen widely recognized attributes of leadership success, the ability to influence others ranked eighth (see table 7.2). Just as with the state licensing boards, the ability to influence others was not seen as a high priority or high-impact leadership skill.

This lack of recognition of the power and importance of influence seems to cross all geographic regions of the country as well as all levels within the organization. There is no one region of the country that tends to emphasize the importance of influence more than any other region. There is no level of leadership within the K-12 hierarchy that tends to place a greater value on the importance of influence than any other level of leadership, from beginning assistant principal to experienced superintendent.

THE INFLUENTIAL CHARISMATIC

For the charismatic leader, influence is critical to success. Perhaps only behind the ability to identify a mission that matters, a mission that resonates in an emotional and symbolic way with others, is the ability to influence.

A powerful mission with no followers or believers in the mission is no mission at all. It is the followers who actually give the mission the voice, the

Table 7.2.   Educational Leader Survey of Leadership Attributes' Importance for Success

Attribute	Ranking
Ethical	1
Trustworthy	2
Communicator	3
Mission Driven	4
Competent	5
Collaborator	6
Decision Maker	7
Influential	**8**
Developer of Others	9
Confident	10
Results Oriented	11
Change Agent	12
Skilled Manager	13
Likable	14
Energetic	15

momentum, to succeed. It is the ability to influence in profound ways that allows the charismatic leader to attract and build that base of loyal believers.

In short, there is no such thing as a noninfluential charismatic. One could argue that a charismatic figure who has no ability to influence others would best be described by others as a lunatic.

It is the ability to influence that connects the charismatic leader with others and moves what might at first appear to be wild dreams or ideas, dreams like going to the moon or imagining a society where everyone is judged by their character, into missions that matter and can be accomplished.

Chapter Eight

Energy Prioritized

INTRODUCTION

Leadership is hard work. It is assumed by almost everyone in an organization that the leader is the one who, with all of the responsibilities and pressures of the job, should be putting in significant hours on the job and be able to demonstrate consistently high levels of energy. In fact, if a leader is viewed as lazy, or is seen as talking the talk but not walking the walk, that leader's credibility will rapidly fall.

Stakeholders in and out of the organization will begin to feel abandoned by the leader. Stakeholders will question why they should care and exert effort if the leader doesn't seem willing to exert the effort necessary or expected from the group. In this case, it will be only a short time before that leader's overall effectiveness falters and the leader is replaced. Simply put, energy is a prerequisite for leadership success.

In the field of P-12 education, where resources are short and expectations are high, the need for leaders at every level of the system to demonstrate the energy needed to accomplish the job is particularly important. A classroom teacher, assistant principal, or principal who is low energy is very unlikely to motivate others to commit significant amounts of energy to the job.

In many ways the attribute of leadership energy is assumed by those who hire, train, and evaluate leaders as a given. Very little formal attention is paid by state departments of education to this leadership attribute. The missing nature of the charismatic attribute of energy in state licensing will be discussed later in this chapter.

The good news is that, with very few exceptions, educators are by nature high-energy individuals. Educators arrive to work early, stay late, and take their work home with them. For most educators, their work is not a job, it is

73

a lifestyle. For most high-performing education leaders, the forty-hour work week has arrived by Thursday, if not earlier.

The charismatic attribute of energy already exists within every successful educator. The charismatic leader, however, is able to combine that high level of energy with the other attributes of charisma. When these high levels of energy are sustained over time, it becomes evident to all stakeholders that there is a high degree of leader commitment to the work, to the mission. When that commitment is combined with the other attributes of charisma, that commitment, that energy, becomes a charismatic force.

CHARISMATIC ENERGY

While there is a great deal of research that indicates that physical features such as height, perceived attractiveness, and gender play a role in the attention that certain leaders receive, it is primarily the charismatic leader's ability and willingness to expend an inordinate amount of energy to attract the attention of followers to the leader and the leader's mission that signals to followers that a charismatic leader is emerging.

While all leadership roles require energy from the leader, both physical and emotional, in order to be successful in the role, there is a commitment of energy that clearly is unique to charismatic leaders. Charismatic individuals consistently display the highest levels of energy (Awamleh and Gardner, 1999; Bromley and Kirschner-Bromley, 2007; Conger, 2015).

There is a kind of relentless pursuit toward the leader's objectives, whatever those objectives may be, that exists within every charismatic. This energy does not go unnoticed by those who are attracted to the leader and the leader's message. Where other leaders may demonstrate energy around a single task or only when dealing with missions that the leader deems important, charismatic leaders display energy, it seems to the follower, at all times.

The energy of the charismatic also begins to serve as a motivator for others. Attention is drawn to the leader simply by the virtue of the extended and unusual amount of energy, of commitment, the leader is demonstrating. Followers become curious and interested about the leader and the leader's motivations.

This energy begins to serve as an influencer, or perhaps more accurately as a producer, of follower energy. As the energy and commitment of the leader rises, the energy and commitment of the follower rises. This energy and passion are therefore displayed by the charismatic individual in their capacity as a leader, or as follower.

High levels of sustained energy also convey the urgency of the challenge or opportunity being faced, as well as the ability to articulate and commit to a path forward (Awamleh and Gardner, 1999). Charismatic leaders are more likely to rise in times of crisis or when followers believe that there are very significant decisions to be made. Charismatic energy suggests to followers that the leader recognizes the crisis or the significance of the moment.

The energy of the charismatic leader serves as a motivator for those who follow the leader. For the charismatic leader, a relentless commitment to the mission manifests itself to others as an unwavering and tireless effort to accomplish a goal. For example, Great Britain's prime minister Winston Churchill believed that the attribute of continuous effort, not strength or intelligence, was the key for unlocking leadership potential.

When colleagues and the community at large see someone going above and beyond the call of duty for a cause, that effort can motivate others. When the leader demonstrates the ability to generate and maintain the great deal of energy needed to attract and keep the attention of followers, the leader is more likely to have those followers commit to the same level of energy and support for the leader and the leader's mission. A motivated team is a team that is willing to commit the effort necessary to accomplish difficult tasks (RoBnagel, 2017).

Like the other standards that charismatics possess, the attribute of effort, when separated from the other charismatic standards, is not sufficient for charisma to emerge. The leader's effort must also be aligned with a belief by the leader, and trust from the leader's followers, that the competence, integrity, and mission are there as well.

This energy and passion for the work is used by the charismatic leader to convey the urgency of the challenge or opportunity being faced. When that energy is combined with the ability to articulate a path forward regarding what collective response is needed, a charismatic leader-follower relationship begins to emerge (Awamleh and Gardner, 1999).

If all educators, or at least all successful educators, bring high levels of energy to their work each day, why are more educators not seen as charismatic by others? High-energy educators are ubiquitous, charismatic educators are not.

The answer to this discrepancy is not found by examining whether or not the individual brings significant amounts of energy to bear on the job, but in examining what the job is that the individual is so energetic about. The question is not Does the individual have energy? The question is Does the individual have energy for what matters?

ENERGY FOR WHAT MATTERS

As discussed in chapter 1, all education leaders wear many hats and must deal successfully with many leadership tiers. These tiers of leadership include the leader as a high-performing manager (tier 1), the leader as an expert in the field of teaching and learning (tier 2), the leader as mission driven (tier 3), and the leader as a charismatic force (tier 4). Each of these leadership responsibilities takes time and energy.

Each of these leadership tiers is important. Without the preceding tier functioning smoothly, it is not possible for the next tier to function smoothly. Teachers cannot teach and students cannot learn in environments that are not well managed (tier 1). Professional growth and ongoing teacher and stakeholder support cannot occur in environments where the leader is not a pedagogical expert (tier 2).

And finally, in volatile, uncertain, complex, and ambiguous (VUCA) educational environments, as exist in the education sector, leadership focus on missions that matter cannot occur if the leader is bogged down in tier 1 and tier 2 activity.

The challenge for the leader wishing to take advantage of the power of charisma is to develop strategies and teams of leaders who can help support the management and technical aspects of the school or district, thus freeing up time and energy for the leader to focus more on tier 3 and tier 4 activities.

Energy clearly must be spent on daily operations. Energy must be spent on ensuring that teachers have the resources and necessary skills to teach and that students have the opportunity to learn. When a lot of energy is being spent on reactive firefighting or conflict resolution and bureaucratic functions, by definition the leader is limited in the time and energy that can be focused on tier 3 and tier 4 activities.

If too much energy is used up on these tier 1 and tier 2 leadership responsibilities, it leaves the leader without the energy to sustain or demonstrate charismatic leadership behaviors. As a result, the energy needed to influence others, to commit to building an emotional connection between the leader, the followers, and the mission, or the energy needed to clearly articulate a powerful charismatic mission is simply no longer available to the leader.

Charismatic energy is, in a very real way, a matter of prioritizing how the leader spends the day's energy. It is said that leaders prioritize what is most valued. To see where the leader's priorities are just look at the leader's calendar and activities. This is where the leader is expending energy.

Does the leader's day represent time and energy spent on building trust and influencing others? Does the leader use emotion and symbolism to connect others to the leader's mission, or is the leader's energy focused on daily operations, conflict resolution, or bureaucratic functions? The answer to these questions leads to the answer of whether or not the leader is operating in a capacity and focusing their energy on behaviors that can generate a charismatic response from others.

ENERGY—ANOTHER MISSING STANDARD

Like the charismatic standard of confidence, energy is another charismatic standard that is rarely addressed and assessed by state leadership licensing agencies. Only five states cover this standard as part of their licensing process for school district leaders. Those states are California, Louisiana, Maine, North Carolina, and Utah. Only the charismatic attribute of confidence has fewer states explicitly examining the attribute as part of school leadership licensure.

For the vast majority of the leadership licensing bodies in the United States, there is no assessment of, or even acknowledgment of, energy as a critical attribute for leadership success. Why is the charismatic attribute of energy so rarely assessed as a key leadership attribute?

One might argue that this attribute is taken for granted. It would be easy to assume that no one can reach a leadership position without demonstrating the attribute of energy. Perhaps the charismatic attribute of energy is not taught or assessed because it is a given that all leaders possess energy in abundance.

Yet, the same could be said for other fundamental leadership attributes, such as integrity. If those who train, assess, and license leaders take for granted that all leaders bring the proper amount of energy to their work each day, it could just as easily be assumed that these same leaders will bring integrity and ethics to the job each day.

This is not the case, however. Integrity is one of the most commonly assessed leadership attributes in the country. It is not taken for granted as a given attribute that leaders possess.

Leadership licensing agencies assess the standard of leadership integrity in forty-six of the fifty states. Only Colorado, Minnesota, Nevada, and Washington are silent on this attribute. Only the charismatic attribute of mission is more highly assessed, with forty-nine of the fifty states assessing leadership and mission.

While it is reasonable to assume that the attribute for energy is, in fact, taken for granted as a given leadership prerequisite, it is also likely that the importance of energy, and the impact that energy can have on influencing others, is not clearly understood and recognized in the field.

It may also be underassessed because there is a subconscious belief that energy is either something one has or doesn't have. If that is the case, energy would not be something that could be taught or improved with knowledge and practice.

When it comes to improving the capacity of leaders to have a significant impact and focus on charismatic missions for their organization, the study of energy provides a great opportunity for those training and assessing future leaders.

CHARISMATIC ENERGY: AN OPPORTUNITY AWAITS

What are the implications for the lack of attention to energy by those who license, train, and support school leaders? If energy as a leadership skill is not something that is assessed by licensing agencies, if energy is not something seen as needing to be monitored or enhanced though ongoing professional development, the trap of leadership energy focused on tier 1 and tier 2 leadership behaviors will continue.

It is reasonable to believe that leaders as a group are energetic. Our schools are filled with educators working tirelessly each day. Our schools and school districts are run by dedicated leaders who do not lack in commitment or effort. When these educators and leaders' efforts, however, are bogged down in daily operations and regulatory compliance issues, all of that commitment and energy is underutilized at best or wasted at worst.

Energy spent on management activities is far removed from having a charismatic impact on others. Sooner or later, the leader's energy, as well as the energy of followers, will begin to fade if all of that energy does not result in profound mission-driven achievements.

Sooner or later the leader and the follower become burned out, become compliant to the status quo. This loss of energy, of enthusiasm for the leader or the leader's cause, is not necessarily a function of time, but a function of attitude. There is a kind of self-fulfilling prophecy between energy and mission. The bolder and more powerful the mission, the more energy one is willing to exert to accomplish the mission.

This loss of interest occurs not because the individual lacks energy, but because the individual finds no emotional connection to the work that the energy is spent on. This is how burnout occurs. The burned-out leader doesn't run out of energy, the burned-out leader runs out of purpose.

There is a price to pay regarding the education sector's silence on energy as a leadership attribute that requires training, monitoring, and reflection. The education sector can no longer just assume that every leader has the energy, or more importantly, has their energy focused on the missions that matter.

The price of misfocused energy is steep. The price can be seen in the ever-shortening careers of educators at every level. The education sector finds itself in an environment with chronic and growing teacher shortages (Betancourt, 2020). The education sector finds itself in an environment with declining numbers of educators remaining in the profession (Sutcher, Darling-Hammond, and Carver-Thomas, 2016). All of the energy in the world cannot compensate for work that lacks meaning and purpose.

Most importantly, the price of taking mission-driven energy for granted can be seen in the loss of potential that occurs when all of the energy spent by countless educators each day is far removed from the charismatic energy that occurs when emotion, confidence, trust, and mission are aligned.

VOICES FROM THE FIELD

The correlation between state licensing criteria for educational leaders and the Sabina and Colwell (2020) study of practicing school and district leaders is replicated in practicing leader attitudes toward energy and effective school leadership. Their study found that the 130 school leaders surveyed ranked the attribute of energy last among the eight identified leadership criteria for charismatic impact.

Consistent with state rankings, these leaders also ranked the attribute of confidence as the next least important attribute for high-performing leadership. This sense that energy is not a particularly important leadership attribute is also shared by those who have significant roles as followers, those in the educational hierarchy who work in the middle of the organization and report to leaders.

Educators with specific roles as followers of leaders, such as assistant principals, department chairs, and the like, also rank the attribute of energy as the least important charismatic attribute a leader can have. It appears that by any of the criteria studied, state licensing efforts, leadership ranking, or followership ranking, the attribute of energy as a key for leadership excellence is not highly regarded.

THE ENERGETIC CHARISMATIC

In many ways, the attribute of leadership energy is a synonym for leader passion. People want to spend time on those things that matter to them most.

When given the opportunity to choose how to spend time, people want to spend that time on tasks that they feel good about, that they are competent in, and that are meaningful to them in some way. The more flexible time that any individual spends on any given pursuit is an indicator of what that individual cares about the most.

The same is true for leaders. When given the choice, leaders are going to prioritize their time around what they believe is the most important work or the work that the leader cares about the most. When the leader demonstrates a kind of obsession for that work, that passion is recognized by others.

Effective and impactful leaders are passionate about their work (Bennis, 1999). That passion can be easily seen by the amount of time and energy that the leader devotes to the mission. That passion indicates more than a purpose, it indicates a purpose worth committing to, worth fighting for.

In the VUCA world of the modern education sector, it is energy that fosters commitment. It is energy that influences and motivates. It is energy that fosters creativity (Atwater and Carmeli, 2009). In environments in crisis, or environments dealing with uncertainty and volatility, the ability to lead teams motivated and working in creative ways to solve complex problems is critical.

The energetic charismatic recognizes the powerful role that energy plays in building and sustaining employee motivation. The charismatic leader uses energy as an important tool to unite stakeholders around difficult, but important, missions.

Perhaps the lack of attention to this critical component of charismatic leadership by both current leader practitioners and those who train and assess new leaders is one reason why charismatic leadership is viewed as something unusual or even unique rather than as a common attribute of all high-performing leaders.

What is certain is that leadership energy focused on powerful missions matters. The charismatic leader is all-in on these audacious missions and demonstrates that passion, that commitment, with a seemingly unending supply of energy.

Chapter Nine

Confidence

It Can Be Done

INTRODUCTION

A fundamental question that every leader should ask themselves is this: Why should anyone be led by me? Why should any leader be followed in the first place? Many leaders assume that the power bestowed by the position itself should warrant a loyal following and never even consider the question or what the answer would, or should, be.

Others may believe that because the leader has clearly demonstrated a level of expertise to handle the job that followership should naturally occur. These leaders believe that it must be evident to everyone what the attributes are that the leader possesses that warrant following.

For many followers, neither position power or evidence of expertise is enough to generate a commitment to the leader and the leader's objectives. For many followers, it is the mission itself that the leader articulates, and the belief by those followers that the leader has the competence and the confidence to achieve that mission, that matters most.

All successful leaders have confidence. That is not to say that leaders never have doubts or question whether or not success will ultimately occur. These doubts, however, are used by the high-impact leader to self-reflect and drive an even greater level of leader commitment, energy, and strategic planning. These doubts do not overwhelm the leaders' ability to maintain a strong sense of belief in themselves and their own ability to meet the demands and responsibilities of leadership.

Why should anyone follow a leader who does not ultimately believe in their own ability? How can a leader influence and motivate followers to reach their potential if leaders do not see that same potential for excellence in themselves?

In addition to being highly skilled in management, technical expertise, and people skills, leaders also need to be able to develop and believe in their own self-efficacy. In this context, self-efficacy is a leader's belief in their ability to exercise control and command over their own level of functioning and over all of the events that will impact each day's work and relationships (Bandura, 1993).

The ability to believe in oneself is critical to success and impact at all levels of the organization. Research by Gibson and Dembo (1984) and Goddard, Hoy, and Woolfolk Hoy (2000) on the relationship between teacher impact and teacher self-efficacy shows clear correlations between the degrees to which teachers demonstrate self-efficacy and the quality of work produced. Educators with high levels of confidence set high goals for themselves, are persistent in their work, and do not give up when faced with setbacks or adversity.

The same is true for leaders in the organization. It is the leader's belief in their ability to accomplish their goals that has impact. Leaders who believe in their mission but not in themselves will not succeed. Leaders who believe in themselves but do not have a mission, a vison, to articulate will also ultimately fail.

FROM CONFIDENCE TO CHARISMA

Like all successful leaders, charismatic leaders must be confident in their ability to accomplish the mission. What then separates the leader who is truly confident in their ability and demonstrates that competence on a daily basis but who is not viewed as a charismatic figure from one who is? Every organization has many highly confident leaders at all levels of the system.

Only a few of these individuals, however, are seen by others as charismatic figures. Leaders who demonstrate charismatic confidence radiate confidence about the righteousness of their cause and their ability to accomplish the goals of the leader and the group (Tucker, 1970). Kohut (1978) maintains that for leaders to demonstrate charisma they must also demonstrate an unshakable self-confidence and voice their mission and their abilities with absolute certainty.

In and of itself, high levels of leadership confidence do not automatically equate with charisma. It is true that confidence is one of many prerequisites for the charismatic leader. Confidence is necessary, but not sufficient, however, for the leader to be seen as possessing charismatic attributes. For leaders who are demonstrating confidence to be seen as truly charismatic in nature, two additional important variables must also exist.

First, as discussed throughout this book, all of the other attributes of charisma must also be present in the leader. Charisma is the sum of the attributes of emotion, trust, competence, influence, energy, confidence, mission, and integrity. Highly confident leaders are not charismatic simply because they are confident any more than the highly trusted leader, or the highly competent leader, is seen as charismatic simply because they possess the attributes of trust or competence. This symbiotic nature of charismatic attributes is discussed further in chapter 15.

Second, it is what the leader is confident about that matters more than the confidence itself. In other words, it is not just that the leader is highly confident, it is that the leader is highly confident about something special, something unique. For charismatic confidence to occur, a charismatic mission must be in place.

When a leader, or for that matter any individual, is highly confident in their ability to accomplish a routine task, that confidence may very well be true and recognized by others. People admire those who take great pride in their work regardless of the nature of the work itself.

Expert power also matters in leadership responsibilities regardless of the leadership tier that task is associated with. Every task requires the appropriate level of expertise to accomplish. The more complex the task, the more expertise is needed. Task complexity does not, in and of itself, however, equate with a charismatic effect on others.

The fact that the confidence is centered on an ordinary mission, in and of itself, removes the charismatic quality of that confidence. A leader who is responsible for designing a complex high school master schedule, for example, may have all of the skills and expertise needed to build that schedule.

The confidence the leader has is evident to all involved. In fact, that confidence is shared with colleagues. Not only does the leader have the utmost confidence that the task can be accomplished, so too does everyone associated with the leader.

There is, however, no charismatic attribute associated with that leader's confidence in the ability to accomplish building the schedule for the school. This is due to the direct correlation between both confidence and mission as charismatic attributes.

Charismatic leaders must also be seen as having the appropriate degree of expertise, of competence, to accomplish the bold and audacious mission. When the mission itself is charismatic in nature and the leader also demonstrates great confidence in the ability to accomplish the mission, then, and only then is confidence an attribute of charisma. Charismatic confidence depends on the answer to the question . . . confident about what?

CONFIDENT ABOUT WHAT?

Charismatic confidence manifests itself as a form of charismatic leadership when conventional thinking would dictate that the mission is too daunting, too difficult for one to ever have the confidence that it can be achieved. It is the fact that the leader is confident in their ability to achieve the mission despite the likelihood that under normal circumstances the mission would appear to be impossible that inspires.

The charismatic leader has a belief in their ability to reach previously unattainable goals. In fact, the more far-fetched, the more scope and audacity the mission requires, the more a type of magical thinking is required to even believe in the possibility of success, the more charismatic the leader will appear. It is the big leap that inspires not only the leader but the followers.

Charismatic leaders have an almost unlimited sense of confidence in themselves and in their own abilities. These leaders do not see themselves as limited by education, by experience, or by specific sets of expertise, but as possessing a clear understanding of what might be accomplished and of their ability to motivate and influence others to follow. The leader's ability to also motivate others to believe in their own ability is one of the core competencies that make up the charismatic leader.

Elon Musk and Tesla provide a good example of this attribute of charismatic confidence emerging from a bold and improbable mission. Musk articulates a charismatic mission, to transform the entire energy sector, from automobiles to the electric grid of the world, from a fossil-based system to a green energy system.

He brings zero experience to either the automotive industry or the energy industry. There are no examples of anyone succeeding in this type of transformation on either front in the history of the modern world. There are significant interests—the gas and oil industry, the automotive industry—who are incentivized to see him fail.

Yet despite these apparently overwhelming obstacles, Musk presents to the public, as well as to his colleagues, an unwavering confidence in the righteousness of the mission and, of equal importance, the confidence to accomplish the goal. Musk appears to be genuinely confident about something that appears to not warrant that confidence. That is charismatic confidence.

CONFIDENCE: ARROGANCE OR HUMILITY

The adjectives charismatic and humble could easily be viewed as opposites. The charismatic individual seems to project a larger-than-life personality.

Charismatics are often described as extroverts, as people with large egos. When thinking about the charismatic attributes of confidence and energy, it is easy to see why the typical descriptor of a charismatic leader would not include the word humble.

This is partially due to the confusion between the two primary types of charismatic personalities, the personalized charismatic and the socialized charismatic. It is true that the personalized charismatic demonstrates an ego-driven "me"-oriented approach to leadership, as discussed in chapter 15.

The personalized charismatic presents as someone who is uniquely talented and capable of solving the grievances of others. The personalized charismatic presents as a role model for what could be and for what followers should aspire to. The personalized charismatic is, by definition, far from a humble leader. It is this iteration of charisma that many identify as the arrogant leader.

The socialized charismatic can project all of the attributes necessary for charismatic impact and project a truly humble outlook toward leadership. This is largely due to the socialized charismatic leader's focus on the value of the mission, not the importance of the messenger.

The humble messenger, with a larger-than-life mission, is part of what attracts followers. Look at the behavior of Mother Teresa, Gandhi, or Mandela. Few would describe these charismatic leaders as arrogant or ego driven. Most would find inspiration in their commitment to the mission, often at the expense of personal safety and well-being.

In fact, it is the humility combined with the confidence that helps the leader form the emotional connection between leaders and followers and is one of the hallmarks of a charismatic leader. The socialized charismatic demonstrates total commitment to a cause while knowing that they cannot achieve that cause by themselves. It is a primary objective of the socialized charismatic to build the capacity of others, of the team, of the culture as a whole, to achieve the goal.

CONFIDENCE AND BURNOUT

The concept of the "burned-out" employee is ubiquitous and crosses every industry and every level of employment. In the education sector on any given day, someone is witnessing or discussing a teacher, a secretary, or a superintendent who appears to be dissatisfied with the job; the employee is suffering from what is commonly referred to as burnout.

This phenomena is often associated with time on the job. Burnout is not a term typically associated with a new employee or someone who has just taken a new position in the organization. Instead, burnout is seen as something that happens when someone has just been on the job too long. These individuals have lost interest in the job itself over time and no longer appear to care about the quality of their work or the importance of the work itself.

Recent research, however, suggests that burnout is not so much a function of time on the job but a function of personality and attitude (Katz, 2017). Katz's research suggests there is a direct link between the confidence a leader demonstrates and how likely that individual is to suffer from burnout.

In short, the more a leader is truly confident that they know and understand the job and how to do it well, the more the individual feels they have the know-how, the expertise, to accomplish the job. When this happens, an alignment of confidence and job expectation, the less job-related anxiety the leader will face.

One might think that because the charismatic mission is going to be so difficult to achieve that burnout would be a more likely scenario for the charismatic leader than for the management-driven or expert-driven leader. However, when the leader is demonstrating charismatic attributes such as confidence, emotion, energy, mission, and integrity, the likelihood of what would typically be described as burnout simply does not occur.

Charismatic missions may take years or decades to achieve. Many charismatic leaders will not live to see their vision realized. Under these conditions, all of the traditional views of burnout would appear to be in place.

Yet, one of the constant characteristics of the charismatic leader is simply this: the charismatic leader never gives up. The charismatic leader never abandons the mission, or the confidence that the mission can be achieved. This level of confidence is inspiring to others. This level of confidence transfers to followers, who will begin to share this charismatic trait.

VOICES FROM THE FIELD

It is interesting to note that the attribute of leader confidence is not highly valued by state boards of education and their criteria for assessing and licensing education leaders. Sabina and Colwell's (2020) review of state leadership standards found that confidence ranked last out of all of the attributes associated with charismatic leaders. While forty-nine states assess the attribute of mission for leaders, not a single state in the country assesses confidence as a critical leadership attribute.

A study of 130 educators serving at all levels of the education hierarchy examined fifteen common leadership skills and also found that the attribute of confidence had a low ranking. Confidence ranked twelfth out of the fifteen attributes, with only the leadership skills of management, energy, and likability receiving a lower value by those surveyed (Sabina and Colwell, 2020).

Perhaps leadership governing bodies, as well as leaders in the field, take for granted that all leaders simply bring confidence and self-efficacy to the job each day. Like the charismatic attribute of energy, discussed in chapter 8, which also receives very little attention from state boards or practitioners, perhaps educators at all levels see confidence as just a prerequisite that already exists in all leaders and thus does not warrant attention.

For the charismatic leader, however, nothing could be further from the truth. Without confidence, no leader can accomplish a charismatic mission. Without confidence, no follower will trust that the charismatic leader will succeed. Without charismatic confidence by the leader, there cannot be charismatic levels of confidence from followers.

Confidence supports other charismatic attributes as well, such as energy and emotion. It is much easier to maintain a high degree of commitment, of energy, to the work when confidence is high. It is much easier to connect on an emotional level with the value of the work when one is confident that the work can be achieved.

While state boards and practitioners in the field may not recognize the critical role that confidence plays in leadership success, and particularly in the development of charismatic leadership, educators at all levels who recognize the power and potential of charismatic leadership should also recognize the critical role that the attribute of confidence plays in charisma.

Chapter Ten

Tier 4 Missions

INTRODUCTION

All leaders are busy. Regardless of the position in the organization, those working in the education sector in particular must learn to cope with, and excel at, multitasking. School leaders have little time in the workday that is not already fully scheduled with meetings or other mandatory work obligations.

Those working in the middle of the organization in positions like assistant principal, department chair, or grade-level coordinator must balance work obligations as both a leader and a follower. Principals and district administrators are often at work before dawn and don't leave until well into the evening.

The question for education leaders is not whether or not there is enough time to accomplish everything. The answer to that question is clear; there is not. The question is What is the best way to use the time that is available? For charismatic leaders, the answer to that question is very different than for noncharismatic leaders. The answer deals primarily with how leaders view the relative importance of leadership tasks, leadership missions that matter, and leadership charismatic missions.

LEADERSHIP TASKS (TIER 1 MISSIONS)

Schools are large, complex social systems that require highly organized and efficient management in order to operate smoothly. Learning does not occur in environments that are chaotic. Success cannot occur in schools where the limited resources of time, funding, and personnel are not efficiently managed. Teaching and learning are complex endeavors that require clear structures, management policies, and operational protocols at every level of the organization (Tschannen-Moran, 2009).

In addition, school safety must be addressed and maintained at all times. This obligation to ensure the safety of all employees, students, and stakeholders on campus is the first priority of every educator. Student learning will not occur, nor will effective instruction happen, in environments that are fundamentally either physically or emotionally unsafe (Colwell, 2018).

Clearly, for all of these reasons, and many more, the need for effective task management is a prerequisite for organizational success. Every educator, every leader, must learn to use specific strategies to identify, manage, and assess the effectiveness of hundreds of educational tasks, big and small.

These leadership task strategies include the effective use of delegation, the ability to distribute task decision-making authority to others, and the ability to build efficient systems that result in task management being handled successfully the first time so that the same issues don't appear over and over.

For too many educators, it is this level of leadership activity that consumes the majority of the day. The leader as task manager is a familiar figure in most school settings. The tier 1 leader is far removed in terms of how the day is spent and what the overall leadership objectives are from the leader with charismatic attributes. These are leaders that Everard, Morris, and Wilson (2004) describe as leading with a "restricted vision."

The limits of leaders who are primarily task and management experts are clearly recognized today. Leaders of school districts hiring and training school leaders, universities, and licensing agencies recognize that leaders must also attend to, and have a significant impact on, missions that are broader, that have a larger impact on the overall organization, rather than just leading a well-managed and smoothly running operation.

INSTRUCTIONAL LEADERSHIP MISSIONS (TIER 2)

It is commonly understood that the primary mission for all educators centers on ensuring that teaching and learning are occurring. It is understood that all leaders must have expert power in their respective fields.

While school management is necessary for school success, it is not sufficient. For most educational leadership licensing programs as well as the professional development that occurs for leaders already in the field, the mission that receives the most attention is the successful education of the students.

For the last fifty years this mission has dominated education policy and leadership pedagogy. The expert power needed to accomplish this mission is seen as a primary leadership attribute. Instructional leadership is at the core of legislative action and education department rule making (DuFour, 2002).

Sabina and Colwell (2020) found that forty-nine states formally assess leadership ability as instructional mission-driven leaders as part of their licensing protocols. Only the state of Alaska does not explicitly address this issue. No other leadership standard is as widely addressed across the country as the standard built around the leader's ability to accomplish the instructional mission of the school.

Despite the wide recognition by everyone associated with leadership selection and training that school leaders must have expert power and a focus on teaching and learning, as mentioned earlier, many educators are trapped in management leadership activity at the expense of missions that matter such as curriculum and instruction.

Many scholars and practitioners are hard at work developing training and licensing programs focused on addressing this important issue. There are very sound reasons for this focus on the leader as an instructional expert. Schools filled with instructional experts focused on instructional missions certainly are more likely to meet their instructional goals than schools filled only with high-performing managers of daily operations.

The leader who has managed to avoid the trap of becoming a manager only and who has developed the expert power and leadership skills needed to focus on teaching and learning is well on the way to success and impact. However, there is another, much less common, mission focus shared by tier 3 leaders and by charismatic leaders.

INTERPERSONNAL LEADERSHIP MISSIONS (TIER 3)

While most leadership training programs today focus on excellence in leadership management and excellence as an instructional leader, there is an emerging focus on a third tier of leadership attributes centered around the leader as a high-performing interpersonal expert. These are the "soft skills" needed to motivate and support all the stakeholders working toward achieving the organization's goals.

Education is a complex enterprise. No one individual, no matter how skilled, can achieve the missions of the organization alone. In complex systems it takes teams of high-performing individuals working collaboratively toward a common mission for success to occur. The team becomes the fundamental unit for success. The team is where high-performing leaders focus their attention (Senge, 2006).

Tier 1 leaders tend to see their primary purpose as centered on organizing the system to ensure efficiency, productivity, and smooth and clear operational policies and procedures. Tier 2 leaders focus on teaching and learning outcomes. These leaders are instructional experts working to ensure that pedagogical best practices are in place.

The tier 3 leader, however, sees leadership as primarily a collective enterprise (Colwell, 2018). These leaders are focused on what Zenger and Folkman (2002) describe as interpersonal skill competencies such as building relationships, inspiriting and motivating others to high levels of performance, and focusing on collaboration and teamwork.

The tier 3 mission is to focus on distributing leadership authority and responsibility to others in a team on a common mission. These leaders recognize that the behaviors and skills necessary for organizational success can be accessed by anyone in the organization (Kouzes and Posner, 2010). Leadership can be widely distributed throughout the system.

In short, tier 3 leaders are focused on building teams of leaders. The tier 3 leader is also focused on providing the team with the necessary authority, trust, and access to the information needed for the team to accomplish missions that are fundamental to the organization reaching its goals.

The idea of mission meaning is critical to the tier 3 leadership mind-set. The tier 3 attitude toward missions that matter is different from both the tier 1 and the tier 2 mind-set regarding mission importance. It is not that tier 1 tasks are not important: they are. It is certainly not that the tier 2 mission of teaching and learning is not important. After ensuring safety for all, teaching and learning is the primary mission of the school.

The tier 3 leader sees the multitude of daily operation (tier 1) missions, these tasks, as necessary for mission success but not sufficient for mission success. As a result, they place a higher priority on activities that are focused on teaching and learning (tier 2). Importantly, however, the tier 3 leader recognizes that tier 2 teaching and learning success is only enhanced when teams trust in each other and are highly motivated to achieve the goals of the system (tier 3).

In this context, it is the goal of tier 3 leadership to articulate that meaningful mission to a team of leaders using a powerful set of interpersonal skills. The tier 3 leader recognizes that the ability to define the big mission and to develop, influence, and motivate the team to work toward that mission on a daily basis is what separates tier 3 leadership from tier 1 and tier 2 leadership (Colwell, 2018).

CHARISMATIC MISSION (TIER 4)

The charismatic leader represents a fourth tier of leadership. Building upon the intrapersonal skill expertise that all tier 3 leaders possess, the charismatic leader is able to establish a unique and powerful bond between the leader, the team, and the mission.

This movement from missions that matter to missions that are charismatic is a critical component for the emergence of charisma in a leader. When the mission itself begins to take on charismatic qualities for the leader and the followers, the other fundamental attributes of charisma are much more likely to emerge and be sustained.

Individuals involved in charismatic tier 4 missions are more likely to also possess the attributes of emotion, energy, confidence, trust, and the other attributes associated with charismatic personalities. In short, if the mission itself is not charismatic in nature, the likelihood of the other charismatic attributes to be in place and sustainable is greatly reduced.

Tier 2 leaders recognize the fundamental necessity of the mission to teach and learn in school. Tier 3 leaders recognize the fundamental nature of interpersonal relationships to achieve the teaching and learning mission of the school. Tier 4 leaders, however, also recognize the impact of charismatic missions, that is, missions that to most seem to be unattainable. These missions begin as aspirations, as a dream of what could be.

High-performing leaders all have a strong commitment to the organization's mission. This focus on the mission and the use of "mission voice" to lead and motivate stakeholders to be the best they can be on behalf of the mission is a critical leadership orientation. The ability to have that sense of purpose and to communicate that purpose in a powerful and relentless way is an attribute that all high-performing leaders have in common (Zenger and Folkman, 2002).

Charismatic leaders, however, have the ability to also articulate a collective identity tied around shared values and a shared charismatic mission for a better tomorrow (Grabo, Spisak, and van Vugt, 2017). Charismatic leaders recognize that followers need much more than a leader to follow, they also need a reason to follow. What motivates people to strive for greatness, to stretch their capacity, to commit to work that is difficult, is the belief that there is great value in the mission (Colwell, 2018).

Stephen Covey describes this belief in working toward something of significance as working for the "big yes" (Covey, 1989). It is the purpose of the work that brings value to the team. Without a purpose, all work becomes routine at best and drudgery at worst. This "big yes" can, in and of itself, be a very charismatic and motivating force in any organization.

Belief is a powerful motivator of human behavior and commitment. Leaders who believe strongly in a powerful mission and who are able to model that belief in word and deed are seen as charismatic. If the mission that is being articulated has meaning and power, the leader does not need to be a great orator or an extravert.

All charismatic leaders tend to have the ability to connect with followers around a clearly articulated mission that specifically addresses a group of people with common issues. For the charismatic leader, it is the power of an aspirational shared mission that dominates the leader-follower relationship (Liebig, 1991). The charismatic leader is able to connect the seemingly impossible mission and the group through emotional, values-laden communication. Finally, the leader is able to demonstrate a strong sense of commitment to the group and the mission even if it means sacrifice for the leader.

The ability to articulate in a clear yet powerful way the current status of the collective and articulate a path forward that will change the current status of the group is a common trait all charismatic leaders possess.

CHARISMATIC MISSION AND ASPIRATION

When describing the attributes of high-performing individuals, adjectives such as resilience, determination, and grit are commonly used. These characteristics are clearly needed by those working to achieve challenging goals. For those working in VUCA environments such as the education sector, where challenges big and small are a daily occurrence, these attributes are even more important.

Those who display these characteristics are often seen as leading by example. Where others may give up or lose their commitment to the task at hand, those with grit and determination and those who are resilient in the face of adversity are admired. It is part of the American culture, this belief that hard work pays off and will be rewarded.

These characteristics of grit and determination allow the leader to stay committed to the goal at hand. There is a connection to how the leader is viewing the present moment and the challenges being faced and each of these characteristics. When faced with a choice in that moment, a choice is made, a choice to continue, to remain determined, or a choice to withdraw. The charismatic leader shows grit by choosing, in that moment, to stay the course. Perhaps the leader changes strategy or tactics as a response to that moment. The charismatic leader does not, however, give up on the mission.

When a leader commits the energy and commitment to remain resolute where others would not, the leader is demonstrating another critical charismatic attribute that is often overlooked when examining the behaviors of leaders. That attribute is aspiration. The aspiring leader is surely determined and resilient. The aspiring leader certainly has grit. It is aspiration that gives the leader a future orientation toward a charismatic mission.

This focus on what's next, what can be, is critically important to the charismatic leader. There are always missions at hand. There is always a "to do" list. These tasks may very well be critical to the overall operation of the organization. These events, no matter how important, however, are not aspirational in nature. When leaders aspire to something well beyond the status quo, well beyond what is assumed can be done, they are demonstrating a charismatic lean.

Aspiration and mission charisma are closely linked. When the mission that the leader aspires to is viewed as significant by others, as something truly valuable and meaningful, that aspiration becomes a kind of beacon for others to follow. Aspiration becomes inspiration. Inspiration becomes charismatic.

CHARISMATIC MISSIONS: CONNECTNG AND THRIVING

There is a significant difference between *working* in an organization or serving as a member of a team or as a follower of a leader and *connecting* to that same organization, team, or leader. When individuals feel truly connected to their work and the relationships formed around that work, the potential for the individual to become embedded in the mission and the relationships, as well as the ability to feel that one is thriving, rises significantly.

People take action, or not, in large part based on the degree that they believe they are thriving in their work. For those who feel disconnected to the work, soon there will be feelings of being stuck in a rut, of being disconnected. For those who feel they are thriving in the work, however, feelings of well-being, of improving oneself and others, and a sense of vitality will occur.

There is also a very social construct involved in whether or not individuals feel they are thriving in their work (Miller and Stiver, 1997). How one feels about themselves is linked to the dynamics of, and interactions between, the individual and the leader and the individual and the group.

This social dynamic is understood by the charismatic leader and helps explain why charismatic attributes such as trust, emotion, energy, confidence, and mission play a role in the follower's sense of well-being, connectedness, and thriving when serving as part of the charismatic leader's team.

It is very difficult to feel a sense of empowerment and value when connected to routine and mundane tasks. When the mission seems to have real value and real purpose to the individual, the ability to feel connected to the work and the team increases.

This feeling that one is thriving is a subjective experience, and charismatic leaders use the power of emotion and symbolism to make these subjective experiences positive and meaningful. When charismatic leaders demonstrate to others that they themselves are also thriving in the work, they are more apt to enable a sense of thriving by the followers.

Individuals who feel they are thriving in their work also experience a heightened sense of vitality and energy, energy that serves as a critical component of the charismatic nature of the leader and follower. That energy supports the feeling that one is actually doing something of value. Energized individuals are more likely to also feel more confidence in their ability to accomplish the goal (Porath et al., 2012).

There is a symbiotic relationship between energy and confidence. When both energy and confidence in the value of the mission and the ability to accomplish the mission are in place, then a sense of well-being, of thriving in the work or the relationship, can occur.

The individual who is willing to give a great deal to the mission causes connectivity that can be contagious as other individuals see great sacrifices being made and great commitment to the mission. When individuals feel that way, they tend to be more resilient, have more grit. These individuals are less likely to leave the organization or abandon the mission.

When individuals feel disconnected and isolated from the team or the mission, there will be a tendency toward feelings of mediocrity, which can be followed closely with feelings of meaninglessness toward the work. It is not hard to understand why the individual, or the team, loses a sense of purpose. Charismatic attributes such as energy, trust, and competence quickly fall as well.

Institutionalized socialization occurs as a collective experience where everyone comes together around a shared common experience (Van Maanen, Schein, and Staw, 1979). Connectivity to the mission also involves connectivity with others in the organization. When individuals are linked together around a mission that feels like a true fit to both the individual and the team, the willingness to sacrifice for the team and the cause rises.

Once those links have been established, it takes a great deal for them to be broken. When charismatic leader and follower attributes are added, this willingness to sacrifice for the cause is only enhanced. The individuals who are truly connected become embedded in the work and the relationship (Hall, Croom, and Hancock, 2019).

Once the leader and follower are embedded around a common mission, a series of powerful outcomes can be predicted, including the ability of those relationships to be more resistant to mission crisis or shock. Embedded teams have increased capacity to more easily induct new members, have positive regard for each other, and have a heightened sense of purpose and energy toward the work.

VOICES FROM THE FIELD

The analysis of how all fifty state leadership licensing bodies in the United States conducted by Sabina and Colwell (2020) found that the charismatic attribute of mission was the most common attribute of charisma identified and assessed in the country. This is good news, as understanding the power of missions that matter, and how to empower team commitment to those missions, is fundamental to leadership success

Forty-nine of the fifty states explicitly address the leadership attribute of mission as part of their licensing protocols. Only the state of Alaska is silent on this attribute. When it comes to the relative importance of charismatic attributes, as identified by state boards of education, there is no attribute for leadership success more important than the ability to have and share effectively a powerful mission.

Even the attributes of trust and integrity/ethics, so commonly seen as critical for leadership success, are not assessed in as many states as the attribute of mission. For those responsible for licensing educational leaders, the focus on mission, and the ability to share that mission effectively with all stakeholders, is job one.

The connection of the attribute of mission with the attribute of collaboration is also widely seen throughout the state standards. The ability to have a powerful mission is, in and of itself, not enough. That mission must be shared and supported by all stakeholders. For the mission to have the power that comes with the full support of the team, the mission must be collaboratively developed and implemented.

A separate study by Sabina and Colwell (2020) of 130 educational leaders in the field, however, found a slightly lower emphasis on the power of mission as a high-impact attribute for leader success than is evidenced by the degree to which state boards focus on this attribute. These practicing school and district leaders identified the ability to focus on, and share, a powerful mission as the third most important attribute, behind the attributes of integrity/ethics and of trust.

Those surveyed did, however, rank mission as more important for leadership success than the charismatic attributes of competence, influence, confidence, and energy. It is interesting to note that this ranking of the importance of mission remained in the middle of charismatic leadership importance regardless of the leadership position held by those surveyed.

At every level, whether it was a beginning assistant principal or a seasoned principal or district leader, the attribute of mission was valued, but not as highly as the attributes of trust and integrity. While this may be explained when looking at beginning leaders or at leaders who hold relatively low-level positions such as assistant principal, the fact that the highest-ranking leaders in the organization also ranked the power of a mission that matters and is understood and shared throughout the organization lower than all of the state licensing boards is somewhat surprising.

For the charismatic leader, while understanding that every attribute is impacted by every other charismatic attribute, it can be said that the attribute of an aspirational charismatic mission may be the most powerful and important charismatic function of them all. All of the trust, integrity, emotion, influence, and competence in the world cannot lead a team to organizational success if there is no clear mission.

Chapter Eleven

Integrity

The Foundational Standard

INTRODUCTION

Perhaps no other leadership standard, or attribute for charismatic leadership, is more commonly recognized in both the literature on leadership and by those leaders serving in the field as the standard of ethics/integrity. Dwight Eisenhower defined integrity as the "supreme quality for a leader" that without having, no real leadership success would be possible (Kiisel, 2013).

Quinn (2004) identifies the foundational state, the identity of the leader, as more important to leadership success than any specific leadership competencies, behaviors, or position. This ability for the leader to be comfortable in their own skin and to recognize the value of character is a prerequisite for any type of leadership effectiveness (Hesselbein and Shinseki, 2004).

Fogleman (2001) identifies leaders who display the highest levels of integrity as possessing sincerity, consistency, substance, and commitment. These attributes, which are linked to the formation of trust, are also closely linked to charismatic attributes such as mission driven, confidence, and competence.

For leaders to be recognized as having integrity, the leader has to be perceived as being genuine and sincere. Integrity and ethics cannot be faked. Ethical leaders must be consistent in their adherence to a core set of values. Integrity can be defined as always interacting with others in ethical and honorable ways.

If the leader behaves ethically only when it is easy to do so, but abandons those ethical behaviors in times of stress, trust in that leader will quickly be lost. Ethical leaders are also perceived as leaders who demonstrate substance. These leaders are serious about their work and the mission of the organization. They bring the highest levels of energy and commitment to that work each day. That sense of mission and commitment is easily and consistently seen by others.

People with integrity aspire to the highest ethical standards and expect the same behavior of others. They conduct themselves honorably in any situation that may arise. They treat every person with respect and fairness. They are straightforward and forthright, expressing themselves with clarity, so that others always understand what is being communicated. They approach their work with honesty, and having made a commitment, keep their word.

Remember that people will not follow a leader they do not trust. Great leaders, trusted leaders, demonstrate integrity. This trust that the leader will consistently display ethical behavior leads to gaining the confidence of followers. These followers then become dedicated employees, trusted friends, and strong supporters of shared goals.

ETHICS AND INTEGRITY: THE UBIQUITOUS STANDARD

Ethics/integrity is the ubiquitous leadership standard. Ethics/integrity is what Zenger and Folkman (2002) describe as the tent pole that holds up and supports all other recognized attributes for leader success regardless of the leadership tier in which the leader is operating. Without the foundation of ethical leadership, all of the other attributes for leadership success cannot be sustained over time.

Tier 3 leadership is fundamentally about building and sustaining relationships. Tier 4 charismatic leaders build on those relationships to pursue aspirational charismatic missions. How leaders use their power, their influence, and their expertise to shape those relationships is fundamentally a question of ethics and morality.

Ciulla (2004) proposes that the impact of ethical, or nonethical, behavior by leaders carries more weight, is magnified, when looking at a leader's impact on followers and their commitment to the mission.

When leaders behave in ethical ways, the impact of that behavior ripples across the organization's culture. The notion of the leader as a role model can be seen in this view of leadership. The leader sets the ethical tone for the organization. The leader is seen to not just talk the talk but also to walk the walk when it comes to modeling the organization's core beliefs.

Ethical leaders are widely respected by their followers, and those same followers are more likely to increase their own efforts on behalf of the organization (Ofori, 2009). When the leader's behavior is grounded around an ethical core, it is more likely that followers will attempt to adhere to those same core values.

It is clear that Dr. Martin Luther King Jr., for example, adhered to a core value of nonviolent resistance even when confronted directly with violence and arrest. Perhaps just as importantly, his followers did the same thing. When confronted with direct acts of violence, King's followers stayed true to his primary charismatic mission.

The charismatic attributes of energy, emotion, and mission all increase when built upon a foundation of ethical leadership behavior. The fact that King never wavered in his core beliefs and behaviors helped provide the energy and the emotion and the commitment to the mission for his followers.

ETHICS AND THE SOCIALIZED CHARISMATIC

Just as the attribute of ethics serves as the linchpin for all of the leadership attributes for success identified by Zenger and Folkman (2002), so too does the attribute of ethics/integrity serve as the foundation that supports the attributes of socialized charismatic leadership. Ethics and integrity, however, may be the one key charismatic attribute that is not ubiquitous in all charismatic leaders but found only in those charismatic leaders identified by their mission focus as socialized charismatics.

There are many reasons that leaders may fail to maintain ethical behavior. Fear of failure, looking to take shortcuts to get to a goal, rationalizing their behavior that the ends justify the means, arrogance, and just being lazy are common reasons that leaders falter ethically (Fogleman, 2001).

Unfortunately, it just takes one or two ethical lapses to lose the trust of followers that the leader is someone who can be counted on to behave with integrity. Ethics, like trust, may take years to demonstrate but can vanish instantly with one flagrantly unethical act.

When leaders betray the integrity and ethical guidelines they are expected to model, the negative impact of that betrayal also ripples widely throughout the culture. It is rare for leadership ethical lapses to remain secret for long. It is also rare for followers, whose own commitment is to accomplishing the mission in a way that aligns with the followers' own sense of integrity, to remain loyal to an unethical leader.

Why should followers behave in an ethical manner if their leader is clearly violating an agreed-upon code of integrity and ethics. Why should ethical followers follow unethical leaders? This reluctance to follow leaders who lack integrity is particularly the case for socialized charismatic followers, followers who care more about the mission than the leader.

Just as ethical behavior can ripple through an organization, it is not hard to find examples of organizational corruption on a large scale where it appears that the entire leadership team is operating outside ethical or legal norms. Often, these organizations are led by a very different kind of charismatic leader (see chapter 15).

The good news is that the characteristics and behaviors of ethical charismatic leaders differ significantly from the characteristics and behaviors of unethical leaders. The same is true for the behavior of ethical and unethical followers.

The behavior of ethical leaders is overt and quantifiable. Howell and Avolio (1992) identify leadership behaviors such as having a focus on developing the critical thinking and leadership capacity of followers as a core attribute of the ethical leader. This leadership focus on empowering and developing others in the organization, of focusing on building trust and strong interpersonal relationships, is the notion of the servant leader (Van Dierendonck, 2011).

Ethical leaders have as a primary interest the well-being of their organization, their employees, and the overall society as common denominators. These leaders ground their behaviors around an altruistic moral code. When that code is coupled with a powerful mission, the beginning of charismatic leadership can emerge.

Bromley and Kirschner-Bromley (2007) identify integrity, ethics, and a strong moral base as prerequisites for any type of leadership that hopes to be transformational. Hackman and Johnson (1991) identify ethics as a central personality characteristic for all impactful leaders.

Ladkin and Taylor (2010) identify personality characteristics such as clearly and consistently expressing one's true self to others, being self-aware, and being inclined toward a life of purpose and virtue as significant factors that help define the authentic leader. It is that high degree of authenticity that serves as a prerequisite set of attributes that enhances the emergence of the leader as an ethical, socialized charismatic leader.

These ethical leaders all exhibit consistent behaviors around how power is exercised, how leadership and group vision is created, and how followers are communicated with. Ethical socialized charismatic leaders see power as a tool to serve others rather than as an instrument of status or dominance.

The relationship between the leader and follower in ethical charismatic relationships is also markedly different from the leader-follower dynamic in unethical personalized charismatic leader-follower relationships (Howell and Avolio, 1992). The ripple effect across the organization, and all of the organization's stakeholders, of a leader who clearly demonstrates integrity and ethical behavior, particularly during times of stress, is significant.

For the ethical charismatic leader, it is the power of a shared vision that dominates the leader-follower relationship (Liebig, 1991). The goals of those following the leader are as paramount to the followers as is the leader's focus on the mission.

Unethical leaders, by contrast, use their charisma to pursue personal goals rather than group goals. They tend to manipulate, control, and limit the ability of followers to grow and think independently. These leaders are much more likely to use power in an authoritarian fashion to serve personal goals and interests.

The ethical charismatic leader, however, values open two-way communication between the leader and followers and is open to and welcomes critical feedback more than unquestioned loyalty. Where loyalty is expected, it is not loyalty to the leader but loyalty to the mission itself. Where ethical charismatic leaders seek a passion and commitment to the cause, the unethical charismatic leader sees loyalty only through the lens of followers being loyal only to the leader.

The socialized charismatic leader places a high value on the ability for followers to accomplish the mission. Because the mission itself is charismatic, it is aspirational and can only be accomplished when many individuals work together. Ethical charismatic leaders have as a goal the liberation of followers, of developing the capacity of followers to also be leaders and difference makers (DePree, 1990).

When examining the attribute of integrity and leadership, one type of leader, the socialized charismatic, seeks to develop and motivate followers toward an ethical cause while the other type of leader, the personalized charismatic, tends to place the highest priority on followers' loyalty, compliance, and adoration.

Followers of leaders displaying ethical charismatic behaviors are more likely to maintain independent thought and continually analyze the alignment of the leader's words and actions with their own goals and beliefs. These followers will analyze the coherence of the leader's words and deeds to see if they align with the followers' own value system.

When these followers perceive the leader to have both a strong commitment to the mission and a strong ethical code, the followers' perception of the leader as high performing is at its highest. These followers find charismatic leaders who are also morally worthy to be the most effective leaders (Gardner, 2003). These followers are primarily mission-driven followers as discussed in chapter 10. It is the mission that matters most, not the leader of the mission.

In times of crisis, the followers of charismatic leaders displaying an ethical foundation are more likely to rise to the challenge of maintaining the purpose and vision that attracted the followers to the leader initially (Howell and Avolio, 1992). The socialized charismatic leader and follower don't abandon or change the mission when times get tough, they double down on their efforts to achieve the mission.

THE ORGANIZATION AND ETHICS

Charisma, while often explosive and unpredictable, can also be a transforming force (Roberts and Bradley, 1988). Supervisors tasked with selecting leaders need to understand the power of charismatic leadership for both good and evil. Clearly, charismatic leaders have the power to transform organizations in both positive and negative ways.

It is not just leaders and followers, however, who establish cultures built upon an ethical foundation, or built on a foundation that ignores common values and ethical standards. Organizations also have the ability to embody and represent a code of ethics. The organization's culture, the brand, are based upon a commonly agreed-upon set of guiding principles.

It is not hard to find corporations taking specific actions when the behaviors of others, both individually and at the corporate level, display behaviors that are counter to the organization's code of ethics. When these businesses find their names attached, through advertising or other affiliations, with individuals or agencies whose behavior is contrary to their mission or value statement, they are not hesitant to act.

For example, CBS News (2018) reported fifteen separate corporations that pulled their advertising from the Laura Ingraham program on the Fox network following comments made on her program that criticized a survivor from the Parkland High School mass shooting in Florida earlier that year. These corporate responses were almost immediate and not an unusual corporate response in today's values-conscious environment.

Companies from a variety of sectors, including insurance companies, travel companies, restaurant chains, and medical companies to name just a few, reacted quickly by removing their companies from any association with the Ingraham program. These companies not only pulled their advertising, they often explicitly commented on the disconnect between their company values and the values stated on the program that were counter to their mission.

A typical response from these corporations can be found in the statement from Liberty Mutual Insurance, who shared that no additional affiliation would take place between the company and Ms. Ingraham's program because her comments were "inconsistent with our values as a company."

In 2018, a wide range of companies pulled sponsorships and affiliations with a significant number of media programs, political campaigns, and sports teams following the sexual assault scandals that have plagued US Gymnastics and the NRA following the mass school shooting in Florida. All of these actions were taken as a result of a perceived misalignment between the culture, the values and integrity of the companies themselves, and of those with whom they were affiliated.

BUILDING ETHICAL ORGANIZATIONS

Howell and Avolio (1992) identified several factors common in organizations that tend to produce and retain ethical and charismatic leaders. These organizations place a high value on each employee as an individual. These organizations value diverse points of view. These organizations are not looking for "yes men" or for opinions only from those with position power.

These organizations are grounded around a culture of dignity and respect for all and have an established code of ethics and standards that defines how they operate. The public perception regarding the integrity of the brand itself is of the highest importance, more important than even the leaders of the organization.

Whether it is responding to outside threats to the value structure of the organization, as seen with how rapidly companies that value ethical charismatic leaders move to distance themselves from affiliations that prove to be counter to their mission and values, or whether it is an internal threat to the company's values, these companies place a high premium on how they are perceived by the outside world from an ethical standpoint.

Finally, these organizations celebrate, and establish as role models, those individuals who exemplify the ethical code the company seeks to promote. These organizations want their brand associated with specific values that represent their corporate mission and creed. These companies want employees and leaders who exemplify those values.

Since it is clear that charismatic leaders who operate from an ethical socialized framework are likely to encourage and enable followers to unite around the same commitment to ethics and the mission, companies with charismatic ethical leaders are companies that are much more likely to have charismatic ethical followers and employees. Organizations that operate under an ethical code that values each member of the team are much more likely to produce and select charismatic leaders who display ethical conduct and leadership behaviors.

In this sense, the charismatic leader is a reflection of, and developer of, the overall culture and climate of the organization, or the group, itself. Organizations seeking to maintain a culture that values the individual, critical thinking and problem solving, respect for a moral code, and a commitment to achieving positive outcomes are likely to value, develop, and retain charismatic leaders who are aligned to those goals and values.

Organizations or groups without a commitment to critical thought, the value of the individual, and a commitment to some type of greater good are likely to be susceptible to leaders who are charismatic but unethical, to the dark side of charisma. In short, what the leader values is likely to be what the organization values.

VOICES FROM THE FIELD

With a renewed emphasis on integrity and ethics spreading across the corporate spectrum, it is not surprising that the education sector also places a very high value on the leadership attribute of ethics/integrity. Sabina and Colwell's (2020) survey of current school leaders at all levels found that ethics/integrity ranked first out of fifteen widely recognized leadership attributes.

The survey of more than 130 educators at all levels of K-12 education, and in positions from school superintendent to first-year assistant principal, found ethics as the consistently highest ranked attribute for leadership success, followed by the leadership attributes of trust and mission at numbers two and three, respectively.

One could argue that trust between leaders and followers and commitment to mission are closely related to seeing the leader as someone who has integrity and a code of ethics. If the leader is not viewed as trustworthy, the leader will also be viewed as lacking integrity. If the leader is not true to the values of the organization's mission, the leader will also not be seen as trustworthy or ethical.

It is not until the fourth-highest-ranked leadership attribute, the attribute of effective communication, that leadership components unrelated to the values held by the leader show up on the survey.

A review of all fifty state standards for licensing educational leaders by Sabina and Colwell (2020) shows the same dominant ranking of the importance of ethics and integrity in educational leadership. Following the leadership standard of mission, assessed by forty-nine of the fifty states, the standard of integrity/ethics ranked second among all charismatic leadership standards.

Forty-six of the fifty states explicitly address and assess the attribute of leadership/integrity. Only the states of Colorado, Minnesota, Nevada, and Washington are silent on this leadership attribute as part of their assessment and licensing criteria for new school leaders.

A typical focus of the state licensing boards' emphasis on leadership integrity and ethics can be found in the standards for educational leaders adopted by the Professional Standards for Educational Leaders (PSEL) consortium of Arizona, Arkansas, Delaware, Idaho, Maryland, New Jersey, New York, and Vermont. These states identify specific ethical benchmarks across not just one leadership attribute but across multiple leadership standards.

How the leader handles resources, sets expectation, builds culture, shares information, engages with stakeholders, provides direction, models behavior, and establishes norms are all connected explicitly to the leader's ability to demonstrate ethical behavior and integrity in the PSEL framework. All of these leadership behaviors are assessed by these states in an attempt to measure how the leader uses ethics to meet these leadership responsibilities.

THE ETHICAL CHARISMATIC

The ethical leader walks the walk. Stallard (2016) describes the behaviors of leaders such as Stan Gault at Goodyear, who valued thrift as a virtue but also demonstrated and modeled that thriftiness on a daily basis.

Gault ate in the company cafeteria, downsized executive office trappings, and eliminated executive parking. It is important to note that these measures are in a very real way much more symbolic than transformational or impactful on the corporation's bottom line. The behaviors adopted by Gault connect with the rest of the organization on an emotional level more than on a financial level. It is the emotional connection, however, that begins to add a charismatic connection to the values being displayed by the leader.

Other CEOs, such as Dan Amos, chairman and CEO of the insurance company Aflac, the eleven-time recipient of the World's Most Ethical Company Award sponsored by the Ethisphere Institute, a company focused on promoting best practices in business ethics, and Rodney Martin, CEO of Voya Financial, a four-time honoree of the World's Most Ethical Company Award, recognize that there is no real long-term alternative in today's marketplace other than to behave in an ethical manner (Reiss, 2017).

These leaders recognize that leading from a foundation of ethics and values is not only the right way to lead, it is also good for the bottom line of the organization. Operating from this ethical foundation builds relationships, which combines to build trust and commitment from all stakeholders (Reiss, 2017).

As with all charismatic leaders, it is the combination of charismatic attributes, all in play and supporting each other, that results in the formation of charisma. The ethical charismatic clearly demonstrates in word and deed over time, and in a variety of situations and environments, their adherence to a moral code. That foundation allows charismatic attributes such as trust, influence, mission, and energy to emerge as well.

When that commitment to the sanctity of the core values of the leader and the organization are focused on a charismatic mission, the integrity of the leader also becomes charismatic in and of itself. This is often seen when followers describe the leader as inspirational, as a role model, as a hero, as charismatic.

Part III

CHARISMATIC LEADERSHIP
IN ACTION

Chapter Twelve

Charisma

It Can Be Taught

INTRODUCTION

There is nothing new about the idea of leaders needing to be trained and able to demonstrate mastery of a specific set of leadership skills and attributes. Advanced degrees in leadership are offered in universities all across the world. School districts and state boards of education continue to train current and future leaders on how to understand and enhance the skills necessary for successful leadership.

National standards developed in 1996 by multiple organizations, including the Council of Chief State School Officers and the National Governors Association, have been adopted in many states. Every state and the District of Columbia have specific measurable leadership standards that must be demonstrated for licensing purposes.

Clearly, leadership is seen as a profession. Leaders must be assessed, licensed, and go through continuous recertification, just as in any other professional calling. As such, leaders must possess a body of knowledge and a set of skills and attributes in order to be effective.

For example, most states require years of experience in the field before someone can assume a leadership role. Most states require advanced college degrees specializing in leadership training before assuming a leadership role. These are all hallmarks of what makes an occupation a profession. All of this training, assessing, and recertifying is based on a simple assumption: Leadership can be taught.

In addition to initial training and licensing efforts for educational leaders, every state, every institution in the P-12 sector requires some type of ongoing leadership professional development in order to keep current leaders well trained and prepared for the job.

What would be considered state-of-the-art leadership preparation in 1920 is certainly not the same as what would be considered best practice in leadership in 2020. The focus in the last century on training leaders as efficiency experts and managers of complex systems has expanded over the years to include leadership training on instructional frameworks, developing interpersonal skills, focusing on data-driven decision making, and leading organizational change, to name just a few areas of training and focus.

Why does the profession spend so much time, money, and human resources on the teaching of leadership? The sector recognizes the fundamentally important role that leadership plays in the overall success of the organization. School and district leaders play a fundamental role in assuring the overall health and quality of the organization.

Second only to the quality of teachers to make a difference in the lives of students is the quality of the leadership. Research clearly demonstrates the connection between high-performing educational leaders and the overall success of students and teachers. Quality leadership is directly correlated to teacher effectiveness and, as a result, student performance (Huber and Muijs, 2010). Few would question the need to expend resources on ensuring that our leaders represent the best-trained educators in the field.

Leadership success is also tied directly to the ability of the leader to form meaningful interpersonal relationships (Zenger and Folkman, 2002). Barnett and McCormick (2004) have identified connections between the quality of the school environment as a culture for learning with the degree to which leaders and teachers are able to establish positive professional relationships around a common mission.

Leadership skills can be identified, taught, developed through practice, and assessed. It is clear that the quality of the leader matters to the overall well-being of the organization. It is also clear that the capacity of leaders can be enhanced through quality training and professional development.

If a leader needs to improve management skills, then the leader will receive targeted training on the skills that high-performing managers possess. If the leader needs to improve their pedagogical expert power, then the leader will receive targeted training on teaching and learning. For many areas of leadership development, there is a consensus among those who train and license leaders on the knowledge and skills that need to be developed for education leaders.

Few would question the need for leaders to be experts in human resources, instructional leadership and supervision, management and systems planning, school law, school finance, or communications, just to name a few widely taught subdisciplines within the field of educational leadership.

What is missing from many of these college curricula and assessments, however, is a targeted program to assess and improve the ability of leaders to display charismatic attributes of leadership. Universities and state licensing agencies have not adequately addressed the role of charisma in leadership or viewed charisma as something that can be taught.

It is not just that the study of many of the charismatic attributes discussed in this book is missing. For most universities and state licensing agencies, the entire field of study regarding the role and power of charisma itself is missing from the field.

TEACHING AND ASSESSING CHARISMA

Like many of the leadership attributes taken for granted as skills that leaders need to learn and demonstrate, recent research suggests that most of the characteristics that charismatic leaders utilize can also be taught (Avolio, Reichard et al., 2009). Characteristics that charismatic leaders possess, energy, emotion, confidence, trust, influence, and mission, are charismatic behaviors that can be learned (Bromley and Kirschner-Bromley, 2007; Robbins, 1998).

Antonakis, Fenley, and Liechti (2011) conducted studies in the field and in laboratory settings that demonstrated that charismatic attributes can be taught and used effectively by leaders. They based their research around a specific type of charismatic leader, the socialized charismatic. This type of charismatic leader, and the specific relationships between socialized charismatic leaders and their followers, requires the leader and follower to share a common set of ideological values with deep emotional and symbolic power attached to the mission.

Specific verbal and nonverbal charismatic leadership strategies identified in the literature as fundamental components of the socialized charismatic leader's behavior were studied. These charismatic behaviors included the ability for the leader to simplify the message as well as attach emotional symbolism to the message, the ability to display a type of moral imperative and conviction to the mission, the ability to articulate the sentiments of the group as a collective, the ability to demonstrate confidence, and, finally, the ability to set high expectations for everyone involved in the organization.

To the degree that these charismatic attributes can be taught, the researchers hypothesized that charismatic validation of the leader by followers, along with the resulting commitment of followers to the leader and the leader's message, would increase as the leader's ability to demonstrate these charismatic behaviors increased.

While Antonakis, Fenley, and Liechti's (2011) research studied a limited number of charismatic attributes and their sample size was relatively small, they found a positive correlation between leadership training focused on charismatic behaviors and leadership performance outcomes. When leaders are given specific and targeted training on how to improve charismatic behavior and given significant time to practice and receive feedback on those charismatic markers, leader performance and follower satisfaction rise.

TEACHING ENERGY

The concept of teaching energy seems far-fetched. How does one teach energy? Isn't energy something a leader either has or doesn't have? One might imagine teaching about nutrition, proper exercise, and the value of getting a good night's sleep as prerequisites for having the energy necessary to lead. It would be a challenge, however, to find a leadership development program focused on these aspects of leader well-being and preparation.

Examining energy in the context of how it is exercised, for what purposes it is expended, or the impact it has on followers is another, equally important way to look at the role that energy plays in leadership impact.

As with the physical and emotional prerequisites for developing and sustaining energy over time, finding leadership programs that explore how energy is used and how energy can impact others will also be a challenge. Energy is more than just a missing standard in leadership assessment. It is a missing part of the leadership curriculum.

The reality is that the charismatic concept of energy can be developed in many ways. As with all the other attributes that make a leader charismatic, first the leader must be educated on the role that each attribute plays in the development of leadership success.

If leadership preparation programs and leadership licensing and assessing agencies never discuss the role that energy plays in a leader's ability to perform at the highest levels, if the attribute of energy is not examined in the context of how energy is allocated and the costs of using one's energy to focus on tier 1 or tier 2 tasks as opposed to tier 3 or tier 4 tasks, the leader will not be able to focus on the development of that attribute.

Just like all successful leaders, charismatic leaders are also working hard and expending energy; their charismatic energy, however, is focused and purposeful. Colwell (2018) examines leadership in the context of purpose and mission and proposes that leadership and the energy needed to accomplish the leader's tasks are different when examined from the perspective of the task itself.

Simply put, energy spent on tier 1 management tasks and tier 2 instructional tasks (expert power), while important prerequisites for overall leadership success, are not as impactful to the team and the overall mission of the organization as energy spent on tier 3 team-building missions or tier 4 charismatic missions. Too many leaders find themselves trapped in expending large amounts of the energy they have on prerequisite tier 1 and tier 2 leadership activities.

A very hardworking assistant principal summed up how her energy is used by saying, "I have been spending so much time dealing with all the different procedural issues of administration, I was not focusing on the one reason I started my career in education, the student. I have been spending all my time on the functioning of the office and realized that if I had to choose to cut something out it would be the time in the classroom. When I plotted my time, I found out that 67 percent of my day was being spent on managing" (Churms, 2016).

This is a clear example of the leader trapped in tier 1 activity. It is not that the leader is not expending large amounts of energy, it is that the energy is narrowly distributed around management activity. There is a difference between management energy and charismatic energy. That difference is not the amount of energy brought to the work each day but how that energy is prioritized. That difference can be taught and understood.

TEACHING EMOTION

Like the charismatic attribute of energy, the attribute of emotion is also negatively impacted by the same lack of attention in leadership development and leadership licensing organizations. Clearly, emotional well-being is critical for leadership success. Clearly, there are steps that anyone can take to learn about human emotions and how they impact everyone.

State licensing standards do address one aspect of emotion and leadership. In twenty-five states, there is some reference to emotion and leadership responsibility. The focus of that attention, however, is not related to the role that emotion plays in uniting people around a leader or a leader's mission but only in the ability of the leader to meet the emotional needs of others and provide environments where academic, social, and emotional growth can occur.

For example, the Professional Standards for Educational Leaders (PSEL) Consortium, made up of eight states, addresses emotion as a core component in the standards of ethics, care and support for students, community care, and responsibility for the professional community of teachers and staff. What is not connected or addressed in any of the standards is any connection between the use of emotion as a powerful tool to unite stakeholders around a charismatic cause.

What never gets taught is never learned. There is a clear body of research that articulates the powerful role of emotion and symbolism in leadership success. That research needs to be part of the training that all leaders receive. That research needs to be disseminated to practicing leaders in the field.

When the role that symbolism and emotion play in developing tier 4 leaders and followers is clearly understood, it is more likely that both leaders and followers will understand how to harness the power of emotion around the work.

TEACHING CONFIDENCE

All charismatic leaders are supremely confident. The charismatic is confident about the value and righteousness of the mission and is confident that the mission can be accomplished, even in the face of many doubters or long odds for success. This confidence is easily seen by followers. Followers are attracted to the mission, the leader, and to the belief that what the charismatic leader is describing can be achieved.

Confidence builds over time, with practice. When leaders never venture into mission activity, particularly charismatic missions that are bold and audacious, they never have the time, or get the practice needed to build capacity as confident mission-driven leaders. The leader becomes trapped in tier 1 and tier 2 activity. The leader's confidence to do these activities may be very high, and that confidence may very well be evident to stakeholders. The trap for these leaders lies in the limits of the scope of that confidence.

Teaching charismatic confidence must involve teaching leaders the value of charismatic missions. Leadership development in the twenty-first century that is limited to preparing leaders to be expert managers of the systems of the organization or experts in teaching and learning pedagogy is not enough. Providing the education and the practice, and assessing leaders only in these areas, is not enough.

Today's leaders also need to be taught the value of the charismatic mission and provided the education, the training, the practice, and the support to be able to have the confidence to carry out those missions. As a result, teaching charismatic confidence must include mentoring and coaching of leaders by those who can model confidence about charismatic mission success.

TEACHING TRUST

Charismatic leaders trust the value of the mission. It is one reason why charismatic leaders exert so much energy, so much emotion, toward accomplishing the mission. Charismatic followers also trust the mission, particularly the mission articulated by socialized charismatics. As discussed in chapter

15, personalized charismatic leaders and followers tend to place their trust more on the qualities of the leader as more important than the value of any specific mission.

The attribute of trust is a critical component for charisma to emerge. Leithwood and Jantzi (2000) describe the relationship between trust and motivation as critical to any organization's mission success. Harris (2003) and Scribner et al. (2007) connect organization effectiveness directly to the degree to which trust and collaboration is established. Without trust there is no success.

Few leaders currently in the field or those who develop, select, or retain leaders would argue that trust is not one of the primary prerequisites for leadership success. What is trusted between leaders and followers, however, as well as the orientation of that trust, is not as universally agreed upon or implemented in the field.

Socialized charismatic leaders and followers place the highest emphasis on trusting the value of the mission itself. Followers trust in the leader is rooted in trusting that the leader will stay true to the mission. For tier 4 leadership, follower trust in the mission is more important than the leader.

In addition, for too many leaders, the nature of trust is a one-way street. In this environment, the leader begins by asking, and expecting, followers and stakeholders to trust the leader. This is a trusting-up orientation (Colwell, 2018). Trust is not an artifact, a job description, or an assignment that can just be given to others.

Trusting up the organization requires also trusting down the organization. This view of trust as interactional means that real trust is a two-way street that requires specific behaviors from leaders and followers alike. These behaviors must be understood and modeled by leaders and followers. The fact that eighteen state licensing boards are silent on the attribute of trust as a fundamental skill for high-performing leaders is of concern.

Trust is a fundamental component of any healthy relationship. The relationships that are built on foundations of trust are fundamental to the nature of all charismatic relationships. Charismatic leaders trust the value of the mission they aspire to accomplish. Charismatic followers trust the leader as an embodiment of that mission.

TEACHING INFLUENCE

In many ways the teaching of influence is the teaching of the use of, and more importantly the limitations of, position power. It is true that many can be influenced simply by the power of the position. Position power has both real and implied advantages. In its simplest sense, the power of the position can influence without any overt action by those in that position of power.

A memo or a suggestion from a principal or a superintendent, for example, may result in greater influence and compliance than the same memo from someone without any position power. Many leaders tend to rely on the power of the position to serve as the primary basis for influence.

As any sector gets more complex, the effectiveness of position power as the sole tool for influencing others diminishes. The education leader who expects followers to dedicate themselves to the leader's mission simply because someone in power has decreed that that is what should be is a leader who is doomed to failure or mediocrity at best.

Other leaders will rely more on expert power than position power as the primary mechanism for exerting influence. These tier 2 leaders do not rely on the title they hold but on the expertise they bring to the decision-making process.

Developing expertise is time consuming, it takes energy and commitment. For many leaders, the recognition that expert power is superior to position power is never fully understood. Others may recognize the value of developing expertise but are not willing to exert the energy necessary to achieve that status.

For those leaders who do understand, and commit to, becoming inquiring leaders who are committed to lifelong learning, the ability to influence rises. When expert power is connected to a tier 3 team-building mission or a tier 4 aspirational mission, the potential to influence others in profound ways is at its highest potential.

Influence is a critical leadership attribute and a prerequisite for leadership success in modern education environments (Pink, 2012; Rousmaniere, 2013). Yet more than half of the states in America do not call for the teaching and assessing of influence as a necessary component of the modern educational leader skill set.

When only twenty-one states teach leaders how to influence effectively, it is no wonder that so many leaders rely on position power as their primary means to seek compliance and cooperation and so few use expert power or the power of team building and charismatic missions. It is not a coincidence that charismatic leaders see influence as a critical leadership attribute and spend a great deal of energy, emotion, and mission focus on influencing others.

Symbolism, emotion, and energy needed to reach aspirational goals are the charismatic attributes that are used to such great effect, such great influence, by charismatic leaders.

TEACHING MISSION

As discussed in chapter 10, there are many levels of leadership work associated with the concept of mission because there are many levels of mission value. In short, not all missions are created equal. As a result, there is a great variance in follower commitment, energy, and satisfaction depending on the nature of the mission itself.

Most leadership licensing programs spend significant time on training leaders to successfully accomplish their mission. The review of state licensing standards conducted by Sabina and Colwell (2020) identified forty-nine states that address the importance of mission as a leadership attribute. Many of these states tend to focus on the strategies leaders need to develop to accomplish missions more than on the strategies leaders need to develop to identify and prioritize the importance of missions.

Mission standards such as "review the school's mission" or "develop, advocate, and enact a shared mission" (PSEL, 2015), standards for Arizona, Arkansas, Delaware, Idaho, Maryland, New Jersey, New York, and Vermont, address the need for a common mission that is understood and reached but are silent on the differences between the purpose and power of tier 1 and tier 2 missions and tier 3 and tier 4 missions.

How leaders are trained regarding mission success is heavily focused on tier 1 and tier 2 missions. These missions are important. Managing all of the daily systems that make a school or school district function effectively and efficiently is a prerequisite for teaching and learning. Ensuring that quality teaching and learning are occurring and that the necessary support systems are in place to support teachers and learners is also fundamental.

What is missing in many programs and state agencies is a curricular emphasis, and scope and sequence, designed to help leaders understand the importance of the big, bold idea, Covey's (1989) "big yes." It is the mission that connects with followers and stakeholders on an interpersonal level, on an emotional level, that generates the commitment and energy necessary to accomplish charismatic tier 4 missions.

Leaders who are well prepared to accomplish the missions necessary to ensure smooth functioning of daily operations but are not prepared to understand, articulate, and lead teams that can accomplish the overarching missions that matter in the system are unlikely to succeed in VUCA environments.

All missions require leaders to be able to communicate the value of the mission. All missions require the leader to be able to articulate a path forward toward mission success. Finally, all missions require teams of committed and empowered followers. Today's leaders need these mission-building skills added to their professional training regardless of the tier of the mission itself.

At the same time, these attributes will not develop in isolation from a powerful mission. There is a self-sustaining symbiotic relationship between the value of the mission and the level of energy, emotion, and influence that the mission will produce. The nature of these relationships is important and can be taught.

It is these tier 4 missions that generate a charismatic relationship between the leader, the follower, and the mission itself. This is a fundamental concept in the development of a charismatic, tier 4 leader. There is no charisma without a charismatic mission.

A CALL FOR ACTION

There is no doubt that the skills and knowledge needed to be an impactful leader in twenty-first-century schools require the ability to master a complex set of leadership practices and demonstrate those practices consistently in volatile and uncertain environments.

Like other aspects of the P-12 sector, the curriculum used to train new leaders is overcrowded. Why should leadership programs add more to an already overwhelming set of standards and competencies? Why is charisma even worth teaching? Why should practicing educational leaders pay attention to the previously untaught components of charisma and how charisma can impact leadership and follower impact?

The answer to these questions lies in the many examples of leaders who are working as hard as they can and yet feel stuck and frustrated by diminishing results. The answer to these questions lies in the high turnover rate and decreasing tenures of school leaders. The answer is because research demonstrates that there are measurable and strong correlations between highly charismatic leaders and positive leadership outcomes (DeGroot, Kiker, and Cross, 2001; Judge and Piccolo, 2004).

If the attributes that provide charismatic leadership and followership affect can also be taught to leaders, then the potential for developing leaders with greater impact on followers and program goals can be significant. In fact, the more stressed or in crisis an organization or sector is in, the more impactful the charismatic leader can be. Our twenty-first-century schools are stressed environments. These environments are just the kinds of places where charismatic leaders can have the biggest impact.

STATE STANDARDS AND TEACHING CHARISMA: ARE WE EVEN TRYING?

Sabina and Colwell's (2020) analysis of all fifty states in the United States, along with the District of Columbia, to determine which of the eight standards most closely identified with socialized charismatic behavior were explicitly covered by state departments of education leadership assessment systems found some startling results and omissions. (See table 12.1 for a state-by-state breakdown of the socialized charismatic attributes taught and assessed in the United States.)

The data from this analysis reveals no correlation between geographic regions of the country and the likelihood that any one charismatic standard will be addressed. For example, only five states address the socialized charismatic attribute of *energy*. Those states, however, are spread throughout the country,

Table 12.1.   An Analysis of Socialized Charismatic Leadership Attributes Taught and Assessed in the United States

Socialized Charismatic Attribute	States That Do Not Address the Standard
Standard #1: Emotion Addressed by 25 States	Illinois, North Dakota, Rhode Island, Michigan, Wyoming, Alabama, Alaska, Colorado, Florida, Hawaii, Indiana, Iowa, Kansas, Kentucky, Minnesota, Mississippi, Missouri. Nevada, New Hampshire, New Mexico, Oregon, Pennsylvania, South Dakota, Virginia, Wisconsin
Standard #2: Trust Addressed by 32 States	Alabama, Alaska, Colorado, District of Columbia, Iowa, Massachusetts, Minnesota, Missouri, Nevada, New Hampshire, Oklahoma, Pennsylvania, South Carolina, South Dakota, Tennessee, Texas, Washington, West Virginia, Wisconsin
Standard #3: Competence Addressed by 24 States	Illinois, North Dakota, Rhode Island, California, Colorado, Connecticut, Florida, Hawaii, Iowa, Massachusetts, Mississippi, Minnesota, Missouri, Montana, Nevada, New Hampshire, New Mexico, North Carolina, Oregon, Pennsylvania, South Carolina, South Dakota, Tennessee, Texas, Washington, West Virginia
Standard #4: Influence Addressed by 21 States	Arizona, Arkansas, Delaware, Idaho, Maryland, New Jersey, New York, Vermont, California, Colorado, District of Columbia, Florida, Georgia, Indiana, Massachusetts, Minnesota, Missouri, Nebraska, Nevada, New Mexico, Ohio, Oklahoma, Pennsylvania, South Carolina, South Dakota, Tennessee, Texas, Washington, West Virginia, Wisconsin

(continued)

Table 12.1. *(continued)*

Socialized Charismatic Attribute	States That Do Not Address the Standard
Standard #5: Energy Addressed by 5 States	Arizona, Arkansas, Delaware, Idaho, Maryland, New Jersey, New York, Vermont, Illinois, North Dakota, Rhode Island, Michigan, Wyoming, Alabama, Alaska, Colorado, Connecticut, District of Columbia, Florida, Georgia, Hawaii, Indiana, Iowa, Kansas, Kentucky, Massachusetts, Minnesota, Mississippi, Missouri, Montana, Nebraska, Nevada, New Hampshire, New Mexico, Ohio, Oklahoma, Oregon, Pennsylvania, South Carolina, South Dakota, Tennessee, Texas, Virginia, Washington, West Virginia, Wisconsin
Standard #6: Confidence Addressed by 0 States	Arizona, Arkansas, Delaware, Idaho, Maryland, New Jersey, New York, Vermont, Illinois, North Dakota, Rhode Island, Michigan, Wyoming, Alabama, Alaska, California, Colorado, Connecticut, District of Columbia, Florida, Georgia, Hawaii, Indiana, Iowa, Kansas, Kentucky, Louisiana, Maine, Massachusetts, Minnesota, Mississippi, Missouri, Montana, Nebraska, Nevada, New Hampshire, New Mexico, North Carolina, Ohio, Oklahoma, Oregon, Pennsylvania, South Carolina, South Dakota, Tennessee, Texas, Utah, Virginia, Washington, West Virginia, Wisconsin
Standard #7: Mission/ Vision Addressed by 49 States	Alaska
Standard #8: Integrity/ Ethics Addressed by 46 States	Colorado, Minnesota, Nevada, Washington

in the west (California and Utah), the south (Louisiana and North Carolina), and the northeast (Maine).

For those few states that cover only one or two of the charismatic attributes, a similar pattern emerges, with no connection between the location of the state and the fact that the states do not recognize these attributes as significant in the licensing process for school leaders. Of the three states that address only one standard (mission), those states can be found in the west (Colorado), the Midwest (Minnesota), and the southwest (Colorado).

There are four states that address only two (2) standards; in the west (South Dakota), in the Midwest (Missouri), and in the east (Pennsylvania). These states only address the standards of mission and integrity. Also, in the west, only the state of Washington addresses the standards of mission and emotion.

The range in the number of socialized charismatic attributes addressed in state standards also has a great deal of variability. (See table 12.2 for a ranking of the charismatic standards addressed from most often assessed to least).

Table 12.2   US State Rankings of Socialized
Charismatic Standards for Licensure

Socialized Charismatic Attribute	Attribute Ranking
Mission/Vision	1
Integrity/Ethics	2
Trust	3
Emotion	4
Competence	5
Influence	6
Energy	7
Confidence	8

The two charismatic attributes most often assessed by state departments of education are mission, addressed in forty-nine states, and integrity, addressed in forty-six states. On the other end of the spectrum, not a single state addresses the charismatic attribute of confidence, and, as mentioned earlier, only five states address the standard of energy.

Four charismatic attributes can be found in the middle of the state standard spectrum with approximately half of the states in the nation addressing the standard and half omitting the standard. Again, there is no geographic correlation between the states that do not address any particular standard and the states that do address particular standards.

The charismatic attribute of trust is covered in thirty-two state standards. The attribute of emotion is covered in twenty-five states; although, as has been noted, typically this standard examines the degree to which the educator understands the emotions of others and does not focus on the role of emotion in impacting the ability of the educator to be a successful leader. The attribute of competence is covered in twenty-four states, and, finally, the attribute of influence is covered in twenty-one states.

An examination of the individual states to determine which states are most aligned with socialized charismatic attributes and which states are least aligned with these same attributes shows that Louisiana, Maine, and Utah address the most charismatic standards, with all three states addressing every standard but confidence.

Six states address all but two of the charismatic attributes. Connecticut, Hawaii, Kansas, Kentucky, and Montana cover all of the standards with the exception of energy and confidence. North Carolina covers all of the standards with the exception of competence and confidence.

On the other end of the spectrum, there are three states that cover only one standard and omit the remaining charismatic standards. Those states are Colorado, Minnesota, and Nevada, all of whom only cover the charismatic standard of mission. Four states cover only two charismatic standards. Those states are Missouri, Pennsylvania, and South Dakota, which cover only the standards of mission and integrity. Finally, the state of Washington covers only the standards of emotion and mission.

What are the implications for the identification and development of socialized charismatic leadership and followership when the attributes of confidence (zero states), energy (five states), and influence (twenty-one states) are not addressed across the majority of the country?

We can't teach what we are not even putting in our curriculum. Like many aspects of P-12 education, the curricular expectations for those training future school leaders is certainly crowded. That does not, however, mean that a review of the relative value of that curriculum, to understand what is working and what is missing for the twenty-first-century education leader, is not needed.

The education sector is a volatile, uncertain, complex, and ambiguous (VUCA) sector. VUCA environments, in particular, can benefit from charismatic leaders and followers. The standards that lead to charismatic leadership are known and understood.

These standards can be taught and learned. Teaching future leaders, and retraining existing leaders, on the nature and value of these leadership attributes is worthy of addition to the current leadership curricula frameworks.

Chapter Thirteen

Succession Planning

INTRODUCTION

School districts across the United States face a shortage of qualified and willing candidates to assume the role of principal (Russell and Sabina, 2014; Pijanowski, Hewitt, and Brady, 2009; Papa, Lankford, and Wyckoff, 2002). Because of this, many school districts are reacting to these shortages of school-based administrators by beginning in-district programs to recruit and train new leaders.

Most of these district programs are highly centralized at the district level. Because of the tightly controlled and rigid nature of most school systems, there is a standardization of program goals and outcomes.

As a result, school systems often use top-down management from central administration to set the tone for leadership styles and approaches regardless of the individual school. This centralization can result in school systems functioning as one large common system with leaders as interchangeable cogs in the machine (Sabina and Colwell, 2018).

Schneider and Somers (2006) argue that school systems attempting to be highly ordered and rigid in their processes will find themselves unable to then adapt in times of uncertainty and rapid change. As a result they are likely to fail in their efforts and become frozen, too rigid to adapt to change and too layered with bureaucracy to customize leadership selection and succession planning.

PERSON-ENVIRONMENT FIT THEORY

A second way of looking at leadership selection incorporates the concept of person-environment fit theory. Person-environment fit theory has been recognized in educational literature for decades, and it is often used to assess the job strain for individuals who do not fit within their organizations (Edwards, Caplan, and Van Harrison, 1998; Dollard and Metzer, 1999).

The fundamental assumption of person-fit theory is that individual leaders will perform at higher levels and with greater degrees of job satisfaction when there is a match between the attributes of the leader and the needs of the organization that is being led by that leader (Ostroff and Rothausen, 1997). This is a viewpoint that many educators responsible for identifying, recruiting, placing, and retaining educational leaders would agree with.

Sabina (2014) comments that, "Selection is the most important element of this theory, as it is the responsibility of an occupation's managers and staffing departments to select individuals who display characteristics that match the needs of the organization" (p. 68). Selecting leaders that fit within the confines of the organization becomes critical.

Systems adopting the person-environment fit theory, with its emphasis on aligning the attributes of the leader with the attributes needed for the particular environment in which the leader will serve, should also incorporate, as a critical component of the process, an attempt to align leader traits with specific leadership assignments (Sabina and Colwell, 2018).

School superintendents and other senior education leaders who have the responsibility for hiring and placing school leaders into job assignments must recognize that there are significant differences in the leadership attributes needed for different kinds of schools. Leadership planners often look at the level of the placement when considering which candidate is best suited for the job. For example, is this candidate best suited for elementary school or for secondary school?

Those responsible for assigning leaders to schools will also attempt to identify candidate strengths, background, and experience in an attempt to determine how well aligned the candidate is with the perceived needs of the school in which the candidate of choice will be placed. Is the school running smoothly, is it a brand-new school with no existing culture or climate, or is the school in crisis and in need of a quick turnaround should also be considered.

In districts of any size there will be schools that are functioning well, the external community and the internal stakeholders are happy, student achievement is high, parent satisfaction and teacher satisfaction with the school, as currently operating, is good. The overall school climate and culture appears well aligned with the mission and vison of the district.

There will also be schools in which stakeholder satisfaction is low, in which student achievement is not occurring at an acceptable level, in which teachers and parents do not feel successful. These schools are probably experiencing a crisis of both academic performance and school culture.

For these schools, schools that need to be turned around, a very different type of leader may be needed from the leader who can successfully maintain a high-functioning school that does not require systemic change or significant buy-in from stakeholders.

IT IS PERSONAL

The field of educational leadership is replete with widely accepted professional standards, the attributes that successful educational leaders should have. These standards are taught in graduate programs at universities preparing new administrators. These standards are used by states and school districts to license school leaders and provide school leaders with focused professional development.

There is a great deal of consistency in the standards identified by state licensing programs. There is also an emerging emphasis on the leader as someone who not only possesses managerial skill and technical skill but is also seen as an interpersonal expert (Colwell, 2018; Zenger and Folkman, 2002).

State standards focused on the area of interpersonal skills vary and are inconsistent. While charismatic attributes such as integrity, mission, and trust are assessed in more than half of the states in the country, significant charismatic leadership attributes such as energy, influence, and emotion are assessed in less than half of the country or are not assessed at all.

Within this focus area of interpersonal skill is a subset of leadership attributes that is not widely used in leadership training, professional development, or selection processes. This subset consists of the specific and explicit standards that characterize the charismatic leader.

PLANNING FOR THE CHARISMATIC LEADER

The selection process for selecting and placing leaders into positions that will maximize the likelihood for success should include a wide variety of candidate aptitudes and school needs. When examining candidates for leadership succession planning, those responsible for candidate selection should also conduct a thorough analysis of each candidate's abilities in the eight traits manifested by charismatic leaders.

Just as best practice requires teachers to differentiate instruction based on the needs of individual students, so do superintendents, and those responsible to select and place school principals, need to differentiate between leadership skills: those needed to maintain high-performing schools, to open new schools, and to change low-performing schools.

There are many examples of successful leaders who would not describe themselves, or be described by those they lead, as charismatic. The attributes and qualities associated with charismatic leaders are not necessarily a prerequisite for success for all school leaders. In fact, in some environments the charismatic leader may be ill-suited to lead; for example, schools in which the culture is strong and stable.

There are other leaders, however, who are seen by external stakeholders, and definitely seen by their followers, as charismatic leaders. These leaders exhibit specific behaviors and generate specific responses from those they lead. These leaders bring skill sets that can increase the likelihood for follower support around significant change efforts or ambitious missions. Charismatic leaders are able to articulate and transfer to followers a strong belief in the need for a different future, a different reality, from the present reality faced by the followers they attract.

The research is clear that specific behaviors signal followers in ways that inspire trust, confidence, and a belief in the leader to impact the followers' lives (Castelnovo, Popper, and Koren, 2017; Keyes, 2002). This impact on followers does not, however, work with leaders who cannot achieve, or in some cases cannot even successfully describe, the mission the leader is trying to accomplish.

The research also describes a strong correlation between the tendencies for leaders with charismatic abilities to appear when conditions are seen by the community as urgent, in crisis, or in real need for change (Popper, 2014). In times of relative tranquility and satisfaction with the status quo there is less likelihood that charismatic leadership is needed or will emerge. This may be due to the connection between charismatic leadership as a function of change and the desire or willingness of followers to be interested in change.

When considering which candidate is best suited for operating a brand-new school, for example, it is obvious that a new school is neither a school with a well-established and successful academic history and school culture nor a school in crisis. This school requires a leader who can create a brand-new school culture and climate. In this case significant change must occur as every facet of the school begins from a fresh slate.

Schools needing to build culture, redefine existing culture, or deal with a crisis in culture are schools ideally suited for the skill set that charismatic leadership brings. These skills are also often overlooked or misunderstood by those responsible for the selection of leaders and the matching of leadership skills with organizational needs.

Additionally, internal and external stakeholders bring with them the successes and the failures from their previous experiences. New schools or schools with weak cultures are susceptible to a kind of cultural hijacking from a small minority of stakeholders if the leader and leadership team don't have a clear vision of what the organization's culture should be.

Without the clear and compelling charismatic vision of what the future of the school will look like, the likelihood for success with brand-new schools is diminished. When leaders who have the charismatic skills described throughout this book are hired, however, with the specific purpose of building a team centered around a charismatic mission, the likelihood for success is greatly enhanced.

If charismatic leaders tend to function best in environments that require the building of a charismatic mission or the turnaround of a school and school culture in crisis, then the succession planning for leadership in new schools or in schools in crisis requires a different set of leadership skills than the succession planning for leadership in schools that do not require significant change.

Clearly, all leaders must have a set of prerequisites skills and expertise in order to succeed. Managerial skills, technical (pedagogical) skills, and interpersonal skills are needed by every leader. (Colwell, 2018; Zenger and Folkman, 2002). Every school needs educational leaders who are highly skilled in these tiers of leadership.

Charismatic leaders, however, have an additional set of skills that result in a highly magnified focus and commitment in the area of interpersonal skills. This ability to focus on interpersonal skills such as collaboration, teamwork, developing and inspiring others, and relationship building (Zenger and Folkman, 2002) in order to identify and achieve aspirational charismatic missions results in a stronger commitment from followers.

This stronger commitment to bold charismatic missions is a prerequisite for the energy and belief needed by everyone in the school culture if the school is going to turn around, to reconstitute itself as a culture and climate that has a sustained impact on the students. It is this focus on interpersonal skills that charismatic leaders use to develop a charismatic mission-driven culture that can be sustained over time.

For district and state leaders working on building person-fit succession planning models, the specific attributes of the charismatic leader should play a major role in determining which leaders are best suited for building new school cultures or turning around existing cultures that are in crisis. This requires those same leaders to have a clear understanding of the attributes that charismatic leaders possess, as well as the best way to leverage those unique leadership attributes for the overall benefit of the organizations they serve.

CHARISMA CAN BE FOUND ANYWHERE: ARE WE LOOKING?

As with all aspects and tiers of leadership, be it tier 1 managerial expertise, tier 2 pedagogical expertise, tier 3 mission expertise, or tier 4 charismatic impact, there are individuals throughout the organization who have the skills and capabilities to lead but do not have high levels of position power. Successful schools are schools with empowered teams of leaders on a common and meaningful mission.

Leadership and leadership skills at all levels may be widely distributed throughout any organization. These individual leaders are just waiting for a chance to serve others and impact, in positive ways, the primary mission of the school or school district.

Charisma does not require position power. Every educational organization, no matter how big or small, has charismatic leaders working throughout the system. These charismatic individuals possess the energy, the emotion, the competence, the confidence, and, most importantly, the charismatic mission itself, and they are waiting for an invitation to lead.

What are educators missing in terms of charismatic mission success when they don't look for, or recognize, the charismatic individuals who are working at all levels of the organization? What is the cost, to students and teachers alike, of underutilizing and under-recognizing the capacity of the charismatic individuals in the organization?

It would be a rare occurrence to find any educator, at any level, who has not seen firsthand the power that occurs when a teacher makes a real interpersonal connection with a student. The power of that student-teacher relationship is significant. It is the power of the relationship that, in many cases, provides the student with the confidence and the direction to pursue an academic dream.

The same is true for the power of the leader-follower relationship. When leaders and stakeholders unite around a common and meaningful mission, the dreams of the organization itself are more likely to be realized. The charismatic skill sets that work at the individual level between teachers and students also works at the systems level between large groups of stakeholders.

The attributes of charisma—attributes such as mission, emotion, influence, trust, and energy—are the leadership skills that help bring stakeholders together around charismatic missions. The fact that so many of these attributes are not assessed by universities and state boards of education only brings greater attention to the need for everyone involved in education and education leadership to start addressing this important aspect of twenty-first-century leadership.

Chapter Fourteen

The Charismatic Follower

INTRODUCTION

Without followers, leaders don't exist (Colwell, 2018). All leaders have followers. Charismatic leaders tend to demonstrate the ability to influence followers in profound ways through leadership skills that emphasize building and maintaining trust, communication skills, and the use of emotion and mission-driven symbolism. There are also common traits, behaviors, and attitudes that exist with those followers who are attracted to the charismatic leader.

While all charismatic leaders tend to demonstrate specific qualities as discussed throughout this book, there are also common traits, behaviors, and attitudes that exist with those who are attracted to the charismatic leader. In the 1940s, Max Weber, a leading scholar in the field of sociology, identified one common characteristic of the follower as someone who believes deeply in the leader as having extraordinary abilities (Weber, 1946).

Other researchers in the field have identified the tendency for followers to have a sense of safety and security when connected to a charismatic leader (Kets de Vries, 1988) as a primary connector between the leader and the follower.

Shamir, House, and Arthur (1993) identified followers' attraction and devotion to charismatic leaders as resulting from an enhanced sense of self-worth. Recent research connects the follower to the leader based on the follower's belief that the charismatic leader represents, and is a clear and powerful voice for, the follower's values (Castelnovo, Popper, and Koren, 2017).

In this sense, the follower sees the leader as speaking directly to the follower. As a result, an intimate, emotional relationship is formed between the leader and the follower. In many ways, it is the followers who decide which leaders are charismatic and the followers who, in fact, validate the leader as charismatic by accepting the leader as the representative for all that unites the followers as a group with a common purpose in the first place (Keyes, 2002).

The relationship between groups experiencing crisis, uncertainty, or a sense of disconnectedness and the proliferation of charismatic leadership types is also well established (Weber, 1968). During these times, people seek out leaders who can bring a sense of meaning or purpose to their lives. Individuals in crisis, as well as individuals who feel marginalized or powerless in some way, are drawn to leaders who can bring clarity and purpose to their world (Popper, 2014).

The connection between the follower and the leader is charismatic because it is rooted in emotion. For this reason, Antonakis et al. (2016) define charisma specifically in terms of the values, symbols, and emotions that leaders use to connect with their followers.

For the follower of a charismatic leader, an emotional connection is often the first connector. It is the emotional, symbolic connection to the leader that resonates with the follower even more than any intellectual connection (Stutje, 2012). These emotional connections lead to what Castelnovo, Popper, and Koren (2017) describe as "over-imitation" by the followers of charismatic leaders.

The follower, particularly when connected to a group of like-minded individuals, moves beyond being merely influenced by the leader to committing to imitate the leader in word and action. The more competent, committed, and benevolent the follower perceives the leader to be, the more committed the follower becomes to the leader's message and style.

If the leader is seen by followers as willing to sacrifice their own self-interest (think of Nelson Mandela or Martin Luther King Jr. going to jail for their cause, or the military leader leading the charge against the enemy despite great personal risk), the level of follower commitment, of follower imitation, only rises.

THE CHARISMATIC ARISTOCRACY: FIRST FOLLOWERS

All charismatic leaders begin somewhere. Often these leaders emerge from relative obscurity connected to a small but extremely devoted following of early adopters to the leader and the leader's message. These leaders may emerge from any sector of society: religion, politics, business, social justice, or entrepreneurship, to name just a few sectors.

Joosse (2017) explores the development of the follower-leader charismatic relationship as a process in which these early devotees, the early believers, provide a series of crucial support systems for the emerging charismatic leader. These early adopters provide both content support, helping the leader refine the charismatic mission message, as well as serving to shore up the confidence of the leader.

The first tier of the charismatic aristocracy is built around the relationship between the leader and the early adopters. This inner circle helps the leader hone their message, providing the leader with unwavering support and loyalty, demonstrating to the leader that the leader should be totally confident in their place at the top of a charismatic aristocracy.

Before the next level of followership can emerge, those bystanders who are curious and interested but unsure if they want to join the movement, there must be more than just a charismatic leader, there must also be a clearly established hyperdevoted group of core followers.

A leader with no followers is not a leader. Individuals attempting to lead where no one will follow are often viewed as eccentric at best and as lunatics at worst. The importance of the first followers is critical to the emerging charismatic leader.

This second level of followers, who then emerge, are often just as influenced by the devotion and loyalty of the early adopters as they are by the charismatic leader (Joosse, 2017). These early, highly devoted and influential followers serve as exemplary examples of how the rest of the followers who join the movement should behave.

Friedland (1964) refers to these early adopters as incipient charismatics. They help spur the awareness of the charismatic leader to others. They help the charismatic leader refine the message and the mediums by which the message will be spread. They help refine the content and the "expertise" of the leader. And perhaps most importantly, they become the trusted and loyal lieutenants of the charismatic leader.

FOLLOWERS AND THE GROUP

Of course, it is the initial behavior of the leader that suggests a charismatic force is emerging that draws the early adopters in the first place. These leadership behaviors are the sum of the attributes discussed in chapters 4 through 11. When these attributes are combined, as discussed in chapter 16, they accelerate the formation and success of the charismatic leader and the charismatic followers.

Leadership, after all, is a byproduct of the collective. The charismatic leader is skilled at identifying the shared values or experiences of the group and reflecting and enhancing those group values.

This ability to meet the expectation of followers and identify commonality between the leader and the follower enhances the group's sense of belonging.

By establishing the attributes that unite the group, the charismatic team also has the effect of highlighting the differences between the group and others who are not perceived as sharing the same values or experiences.

For this reason a strong sense of us versus them often develops. The charismatic leader is the reflection of the feeling of the group as a unique social and cultural construct. The group certainly seeks to expand and invite others to join the leader as long as they commit to the leader's mission.

It is the charismatic leader, in this view, who will protect and support the collective against those who do not share the group's values or who mean the group harm. All charismatic leader-follower relationships are built around this sense of group mindedness (Tomasello and Rakoczy, 2003).

THE APPEAL OF THE GROUP

Joosse (2017) describes a kind of "vicarious charisma" that can emerge when unsure or curious followers visit charismatic followers by attending an event held by a charismatic leader. There is an impact on those individuals who show up perhaps just to see what all the fuss is about or to learn more about the leader. This potential next-level follower is interested in the leader but also in the followers who have already committed to the leader and their common interest in the leader's message.

That vicarious impact comes not just from seeing the leader "perform" but also from seeing how the devoted followers behave and react to the leader and the message. These visitors to the charismatic team event will ask themselves, "Why are these people so dedicated and committed to the leader? Why are they so happy and enthralled by the event itself, that they are willing to stand in line for hours just to get the opportunity to see the charismatic leader in person?"

By observing the behaviors of the early adopters, the next tier of followers are learning how to behave, and they are learning what to believe. It is not hard to see why many laypeople may become convinced that they too should join this movement. Joosse (2017) refers to this phenomenon as beginning with a fascination with the fascination. These individuals are what Dawson (2011) refers to as being "charisma hungry."

FOLLOWERS AND LEADERS: TWO-WAY STREETS

While most research on charismatic leadership has a focus on the impact that charismatic leaders have on followers, there is an important, and often neglected, area of research dealing with the impact that followers have on leaders (Howell and Shamir, 2005). Followers clearly are influenced by, and react to, charismatic leaders. The opposite is also true.

Charismatic leaders respond to, and are influenced by, how their followers are behaving. There is a contract that develops between charismatic leaders and charismatic followers, a promise to deliver. Making good on the contract between the leader and the follower requires both parties to do their part.

Howell and Shamir (2005) have identified two fundamental types of charismatic figures and charismatic leader-follower relationships: personalized and socialized. Each of these charismatic leadership and followership types requires specific behaviors from both parties. These behaviors, however, have several unique, and fundamentally important, differences.

It is a trap to see all charismatic leaders as rising from a specific set of specific leadership goals shared by every charismatic individual, all operating at an advanced level. It is a trap to view all charismatic group dynamics, emotions, and affiliations that arise from the group and are given voice and direction by the leader to be emanating from the same noble purpose.

Charismatic leaders and charismatic followers arise not just from a set of leader or follower attributes, but also from the building of a relationship with very strong bonds and commitments from both the leader and the follower. As the group identity grows and is nurtured by the leader, the number of followers grows, as does the charismatic power of the leader (Stutje, 2012).

Whether the follower perceives the leader to be functioning primarily in a personalized framework or a socialized framework will result in very different follower expectations of the leader, however. These follower differences will influence the confidence, effectiveness, and overall ultimate success of the leader. The followers' reactions, for those who are looking for a personalized relationship, will be very different from followers who are looking for a socialized relationship with the leader.

The trust that a follower has in the leader is based in large part on what the expectations are that the follower has in the leader in the first place. Just as important is the trust that the leader has in the follower.

When there is an alignment between what followers are expecting from the leader and what the leader then actually delivers, that trust and commitment between the follower and the leader is enhanced. When the leader is not delivering what the follower is expecting, that trust and commitment declines or disappears altogether. If followers are not delivering what the leader needs to be successful, trust and commitment from the leader is also likely to disappear.

THE SOCIALIZED FOLLOWER-LEADER RELATIONSHIP

This category of charismatic leadership and followership connects leaders and followers, not as a result of a perceived sense of leadership power, fame, or some other form of personal attribute that the follower aspires to connect with, but from a direct connection with the leader's message. These followers typically have strong self-concepts and a specific code of behavior and goals they seek to accomplish for themselves and the group.

These followers are attracted to charismatic missions more that charismatic personalities. These followers connect to the leader's message and the alignment between the values, the mission, of the leader and the followers' own strongly held values and beliefs. These are what House and Howell (1992) describe as socialized followers.

For the socialized follower, the strength of the relationship is directly tied to the degree to which the leader stays on message. As a result, the socialized follower will not follow a leader blindly. If the leader no longer promises, or delivers, on the common values and mission held between the leader and the follower, the follower will abandon the leader (Howell and Shamir, 2005).

The socialized follower does not attribute magical power to the leader, only the ability to passionately and consistently articulate the goals of the follower and the follower's group. The socialized charismatic leader shares many of the same leadership attributes as personalized charismatic leaders' attributes such as energy, competence, influence, and confidence, but first among those attributes is the leader's belief in the sanctity and power of the charismatic mission itself.

As a result, the charismatic leader of socialized followers must attend to a consistent message, connected to the mission itself, if the leader wishes to stay relevant as a leader. The socialized follower, as a result, has a great deal of influence on the behavior of the leader.

When the leader strays from the mission, from the message, the leader loses the follower. The leader must adhere not only to the mission itself but also to the social goals and mores of the group in order to maintain the loyalty and commitment from the group. In a sense, the charismatic leader of socialized followers is a follower of the group also.

In both personalized and socialized charismatic leader-follower relationships, Howell and Shamir (2005) see a two-way street. The more that followers approve of, and support, the leader, the more the leader feels empowered and confident in their approach. The more empowered and confident the leader is in their approach, the more likely it is that followers will provide their support.

For the leader in a personalized relationship, feelings of omnipotence may emerge. For the socialized leader, however, the relationships remain connected to the mission and are thus less likely to result in leadership feelings of grandeur or magical power.

In many ways, it is the follower who validates whether leaders are personalized charismatics or socialized charismatics, by accepting the leader as the representative for all that unites the followers with a common connection, a common purpose, in the first place (Keyes, 2002).

FOLLOWERS AND LEADERS:
THE POLITICS OF THE COMMITTED TEAM

Schools are fundamentally social organizations. People not only run the school system, but people are also the school system's product. In addition, almost everyone has been a product of the school system and as a result feels entitled to an "expert" opinion on how well the organization is functioning.

Add to this the fact that school systems are also publicly funded agencies regulated by multiple local, state, and national agencies and it is easy to understand why schools are also highly political and politicized entities. Education is one of the few sectors in our society where everyone feels they are an expert on the subject.

All school employees, whether in leadership positions, classroom teachers, or support staff, are impacted by the political dynamics in play at any given time in their school, school district, and state. Charismatic leaders are not exempt from political pressure or considerations. In short, leaders must attend to and navigate the political environment just as with the fiscal environment or the academic environment.

How then does the relationship between the charismatic leader and those who follow the leader impact the politics of school leadership? Do followers give charismatic leaders a kind of political cover? Or, does the formation of a charismatic team threaten the status quo of the system or of leaders who are not demonstrating charisma?

The more passionate and committed the follower base is to the leader and the leader's mission, the easier it is for the leader to pursue difficult goals. The size of the follower base is certainly recognized by those who regulate schools or have impact on policy makers. As a result, there is a certain political capital that occurs with large devoted charismatic teams that provides the charismatic leader more time, more resources, and more flexibility to pursue ambitious goals.

There is also more likelihood that those who are insecure in their positions or their methodology may be threatened by what appears to be a wave of change or innovation. Many charismatic leaders and their followers who are now seen as innovators are first seen as disrupters.

That being said, particularly in an age where society expects instant results from educators and patience is not a rewarded virtue, the charismatic follower provides an incredibly valuable resource to the leader. That resource is time, time to remain focused on the big picture, time to survive the inevitable setbacks and stumbling blocks that will always occur when pursuing a bold agenda, and time to build capacity in the organization to achieve the leader's goals.

Not every leader has a strategic vision at all, much less one that rises to the level of a charismatic strategic vision. Research indicates that only 28 percent of school district leaders have a strategic plan when they assume leadership roles (Thessin, 2017). Without a clearly articulated mission and a plan to achieve that mission, it is highly unlikely that followers will appear, much less be able to understand and support the leader.

While a strategic plan is not, in and of itself, charismatic, without a mission and a plan to accomplish that mission, there is no chance that a charismatic energy committed to mission success will emerge from either leaders or their followers.

The unfortunate fact of the matter is that the majority of those in leadership positions are bogged down in tier 1 daily management activity. These leaders are task oriented; they are firefighters. Often, the leader, at any level of the system, is not even aware of how the day is spent (Ammons and Newell, 1989).

These tier 1 leaders know they have been very busy each day. The leader may even know that important tasks were accomplished or significant operational problems solved, but when asked to identify how the day was spent in advancing the primary goals and mission of the organization, the leader truly won't know.

It is hard to be a charismatic leader when bogged down with daily management operations of the classroom, the school, or the school district. Managers don't have followers, they have subordinates. Managers don't find passion in their work because the work itself does not warrant a passionate response. That does not mean the work is not necessary; it certainly is.

Teaching and learning will not occur in unmanaged or poorly managed environments. Cleary, big ideas and transformational initiatives will not occur when the management basics are not well established. It is just as certain that the gathering of followers, and the support of those followers, is needed to navigate the political waters if the leader and the follower want to accomplish more than the maintenance of the status quo. This support requires leaders to be seen as mission driven.

For those leaders who begin their work with a powerful mission-driven agenda and a strategic plan to accomplish that mission, who learn how to harness the power of charisma to focus on charismatic missions, the ability to generate a team of mission-driven followers rises. The likelihood of mission success also rises. The ability to navigate the politics of the education sector increases.

This commitment of leaders and followers united around a common mission is the embodiment of what a successful team looks like. When the team is committed to the mission over the long haul, the team also is more likely to demonstrate the motivation and resilience needed to stay the course.

All of these interactions increase the likelihood for charismatic leadership success. There is a clear symbiotic relationship between the charismatic leader and the charismatic follower. Each benefits from the existence of the other. Each is dependent on the existence of the other.

CHARISMATIC FOLLOWERS

Sabina and Colwell (2020) studied more than 130 educators serving at different levels as leaders and followers across multiple school districts to determine their attitudes toward fifteen standards identified in the literature as impactful for successful leadership (see table 14.1) and successful followership (see table 14.2). Included were the standards identified as prerequisites for socialized charismatic behaviors as examined in this book.

These same educators, serving in the middle of the organization, were then resurveyed after ninety days in order to minimize prior survey bias to determine the degree to which the same socialized charismatic attributes examined, in terms of impact on leadership from the middle of the organization, impacted their ability to be successful high-performing followers.

There was remarkable consistency between the respondents' assessment of the importance of these charismatic attributes when serving as leaders and when serving as followers. What mattered most to those serving as leaders in the organization, with a few exceptions, was the same as what mattered most for those same individuals when serving as followers in the organization.

Integrity/ethics and *trust* were the most important attributes for successful followership, mirroring the results of the earlier leadership survey. These findings also align with the study done by Sabina and Colwell (2020) on the number of state departments of education in the United States that explicitly assess any of the standards that are identified with socialized charismatic leadership.

Table 14.1.　Leadership Attribute Rankings

Attribute	Ranking
* Ethics/Integrity	1
* Trust	2
* Mission	3
Communication	4
* Competency	5
Decision Making	6
Collaboration	7
Results Oriented	8
Change Agent	9
Develop Others	10
* Influence Others	11
* Confidence	12
Management Skills	13
* Energy	14
Likable	15

* Socialized Charismatic Attribute

As mentioned earlier, this study of all state licensing standards for educational leaders found that forty-six out of the fifty states identified integrity/ethics as a critical leadership attribute. Only the charismatic attribute of mission was assessed in more states in the country: forty-nine out of fifty.

While lower in terms of the number of states that identify trust as a required leadership skill, in thirty-two states out of fifty, trust was still the third most cited charismatic leadership attribute assessed in the country. Whether assessed from the perspective of state education departments, leaders in the field who serve at the top of the organizational hierarchy, or those in the field who serve as both leaders and followers, the charismatic attributes of mission, trust, and integrity/ethics were consistently rated as having the highest leadership and followership priority and impact.

While rated relatively high by the respondents for importance in both leadership and followership, mission was rated as more important (third) for successful leadership than for successful followership (fourth). This subtle difference in ranking between when serving as a leader in the middle and serving as a follower in the middle aligns with the notion of the leader needing to represent a clear and compelling mission more so than the follower. At face value, the follower is reacting to the mission that has been identified by the leader rather than developing the mission itself.

The follower survey identified the charismatic attribute of competence with a slightly higher rating (third) when viewed from the position of high-performing follower than from the position of high-performing leader (fourth). It is also rational to see the follower, more than the leader, as needing to demonstrate the competence to carry out delegated tasks.

When serving in the role of leader, the individual is delegating authority to the follower and expects the follower to have the skills and competence to successfully carry out that delegated assignment. Thus, when serving as a leader working from the middle of the organization, the attribute of competence is not as important as when serving as a follower from the middle of the organization.

The charismatic attribute of influence was also rated higher (fifth) when serving as a leader than when serving as a follower (sixth). It would make sense that the leader as an influencer and the follower as someone being influenced also aligns with the traditional roles of leader and follower.

The charismatic attribute of confidence was rated lower (sixth) for impact when serving as a leader than when serving as a follower (fifth). This would seem to be counter to the research that regards leadership confidence as a prerequisite for success.

Energy was seen as the least important attribute for both the leader and the follower. It is interesting to note that, as with the highest rated attributes for leadership and followership, the lowest rated attributes, confidence and energy, also were the least assessed leadership skills by state departments of education with zero states in the country assessing the attribute of confidence and only five states addressing the attribute of energy.

These surveyed educators have all been recognized as high performers and given the responsibility to serve in formal leadership and followership capacities. These educators also serve in districts of all sizes, at all levels of the American education system from kindergarten through high school, and have varied years of experience in the education sector. Their work requires them to constantly shift between leadership and followership roles and responsibilities.

Table 14.2.   Comparison of Rank Order Socialized Charismatic Attributes of Educators Serving as Leaders and Followers from the Middle

Charismatic Attribute	Leader Ranking	Follower Ranking
Integrity/Ethics	1	1
Trust	2	2
Mission/Vision	3	4
Competence	4	3
Influence	5	6
Confidence	6	5
Energy/Emotion	7	7

Despite these differences, the analysis of what attributes make them successful in both capacities shows a clear congruence between successful leadership attributes and successful followership attributes. The socialized charismatic attributes that make one a successful leader are fundamentally the same attributes that make one a successful follower.

Chapter Fifteen

The Dark Side of Charisma

PERSONALIZED CHARISMATIC MISSIONS

History is replete with examples of charismatic leaders who led followers down unethical, dangerous, and immoral paths. This "dark side" of charisma manifests itself in specific ways by both charismatic leaders and followers of charismatic leaders who represent what scholars refer to as the personalized charismatic as opposed to the socialized charismatic.

All charismatic leaders, both socialized and personalized, share many common leadership traits. Both types of charismatics use symbolism and emotion to help connect with followers. Both types of charismatics have high levels of energy and competence. Both types of charismatics are focused on very specific charismatic missions.

There are specific and significant attribute differences, however, between socialized and personalized charismatics as well as for personalized and socialized charismatic followers. Personalized followers are drawn more to the personality and confidence of the leader rather than the leader's message. The personalized follower is more likely to adjust to whatever the leader's message may be, even if that message changes over time.

The charismatic trait of integrity is more closely aligned with socialized charismatic leaders than personalized charismatic leaders. This is perhaps most recognizable when examining the primary mission of the charismatic leader, as charismatic mission orientation is very different between personalized and socialized charismatics. In its simplest terms, the primary mission of the socialized charismatic lies outside the leader.

Think of Martin Luther King Jr.'s mission to bring social justice to the poor and ethnic minorities in the United States, or Nelson Mandela's mission to end apartheid in South Africa. These leaders were prepared to sacrifice themselves for the mission because the mission was more important than they were.

For the personalized charismatic, the notion that'the mission is more important than the leader is not usually the case. It is not that the personalized charismatic does not have a powerful mission that is being articulated and pursued with energy, confidence, and emotion. Like socialized charismatic leaders, those attributes are all in play. The difference is how the personalized charismatic sees him- or herself in the context of the overall mission.

In the case of the personalized charismatic, the leader is not willing to sacrifice themselves for the good of the mission. In fact, personalized leaders see their own well-being and superiority as a charismatic mission unto itself. Once preservation of self at all costs becomes a mission, the ability for the leader to rationalize or ignore unethical behavior grows.

Just as followers follow the lead from ethical leaders regarding what is and is not acceptable ethical behavior, so too do followers of unethical leaders tend to mimic leadership ethics, or lack thereof. If the leader models self-preservation or self-glory as the primary mission, that will be true of the followers. If the leader is capable of acts of evil, so too are the followers who remain loyal to the leader.

The examples of cult leaders, political leaders, or corporate leaders behaving unethically are numerous. So too are the examples of the followers enabling and participating in those same behaviors. Extreme examples of cult-like followers willing to support any behavior or directive from the leader, as in the mass suicide of the followers of Jim Jones in Guyana, are unfortunately all too common.

Large corporations are also not immune from leadership that fails to meet the basic standards of integrity and ethics. Corporations such as Enron Corporation and their scandal in 2001, or more recently the Wells Fargo Bank scandal in 2016, are examples where large groups of enabling followers participated in, and supported, the unethical behavior of corporate leaders.

This personalized leader prizes loyalty from followers above all else. Highly skilled unethical charismatic leaders are able to leave followers with the impression that what they are doing and saying is in the best interests of the follower all the while seeking only to satisfy their own limited self-interests (Howell and Avolio, 1992).

COMPETENCE AND THE PERSONALIZED CHARISMATIC

Before the question of competence as a charismatic prerequisite can be fully understood, the nature of the personalized charismatic leader versus the socialized charismatic leader must be examined. While there are attributes that both socialized and personalized charismatics share—attributes such as energy, emotion, and influence—competency is one of three attributes, along with ethics/integrity and mission, that differ between personalized and socialized charismatics.

Personalized charismatics do not necessarily need to demonstrate the attribute of competence in order to be considered charismatic by others. The perceived success of the personalized charismatic can be so powerful as to mask the degree to which the leader is actually succeeding. Socialized charismatics, on the other hand, do need this attribute to be considered charismatic by others. Failure to demonstrate competence to accomplish the mission can be a fatal flaw for the socialized charismatic.

Because the role of the personalized charismatic is fundamentally self-serving, the need to be competent in some area of external service or skill set is greatly diminished. Because the goal of followers of personalized charismatics is to be just like the leader in words and actions, it often doesn't matter particularly to the follower whether or not the personalized charismatic leader is actually demonstrating competence in any demonstrable way.

The socialized charismatic has a mission that is rooted in some external goal. John F. Kennedy's goal to send a man to the moon is an example of this kind of socialized charismatic external mission-driven orientation. The personalized charismatic, however, has a primary mission that is centered on an internal goal.

The personalized charismatic sees him or herself as special: possessing unique skills and power. The personalized charismatic's mission is to share that specialness with others, to convince others that the best thing for them is to be just like the personalized charismatic by emulating the words and actions of the leader.

The personalized charismatic asks followers to watch, behave like, and support, no matter what the cost, the leader so that they too can be just like the leader. At a minimum, the leader promises, and the followers believe, that their problems will be solved.

This focus on the infallibility of the personalized charismatic leader is often referred to as the dark side of charisma. History is also replete with personalized charismatics who establish cults of personality, or leaders whose actions and belief systems lead to war, to divisions based on real or perceived differences, and to the separation of people into camps of us and them.

Hitler is a relatively recent example of the dark side of charisma, of the personalized charismatic. While the outcomes from some leaders who are personalized charismatic figures and those who are socialized charismatic leaders could not be starker, many of the leadership characteristics that both types of leaders have are the same.

Both types of charismatic leaders have very high levels of energy and use emotion and symbolism as a connector to followers. Both personalized and socialized charismatic leaders have very high degrees of confidence in their ability to accomplish their goals.

Both types of leaders have tremendous capacity to influence others. These leaders are all successful in their messaging. The importance of the leader demonstrating expertise or competence, however, is very different in the relationship between followers and personalized charismatic figures than it is between followers and socialized charismatic figures.

The fact that the personalized charismatic leader has emerged with a powerful message that resonates with other like-minded individuals or individuals who share the grievances articulated by the leader and that the leader has a following is enough. The goal of the follower is to be just like the leader, to believe in what the leader believes in, regardless of what that belief system is. However, whether the leader has a demonstrated level of competence to actually accomplish particular goals is largely irrelevant to the relationship between leader and follower.

EMOTION AND THE PERSONALIZED CHARISMATIC

The benefits of leaders committing on an emotional level to their work enhances the likelihood for them to have a profound impact on the organization and increases the energy, resilience, and grit that they bring to their work. But there is also a danger to leadership that relies solely on the power of emotion and symbolism to persuade and influence others.

One side effect of leading primarily through emotion is the tendency for followers to not think critically about the leader's message and the leader's solutions. This is what Schjoedt et al. (2013) call the ability to regulate for error monitoring. Charismatic leaders may use strategies that connect to emotions, to idealized visons for the future, or exaggerated descriptions of grievances or current status, such as overloading the group with information, mixing actual information with myth or outright incorrect information, or stating opinion as fact.

The more successful the charismatic leader is in convincing followers of the correctness of the leader's current description of reality, and the way forward from that reality, the more likely the follower will be to suspend critical thinking and analysis.

PERSONALIZED FOLLOWERS AND MISSION

The personalized charismatic leader is much more likely to claim origin of the mission than the socialized charismatic leader. Since the primary relationship between personalized followers and leaders is built around the power of the leader at least as much as the power of the leader's mission, where the idea comes from becomes important.

In many ways, supporting the personalized charismatic leader becomes a mission in and of itself for personalized charismatic followers. It is not that the follower does not believe in the mission that the personalized leader espouses. All charismatic leaders are able to articulate a mission that resonates deeply with their followers.

Personalized charismatic leaders do, however, often own the origin of the mission. In this case, the leader claims to have a unique understanding of, and sole responsibility for, defining the mission and articulating the circumstances and metrics by which the mission will be deemed a success.

As a result, for personalized charismatic leaders and their followers, the mission is subservient to the leader. If the leader redefines the mission or the nature of mission success, the personalized charismatic follower adopts to the new mission parameters, definitions, and metrics.

PERSONALIZED FOLLOWERS AND ETHICS

The impact on followers of socialized charismatic leaders is very different from the impact on followers of personalized charismatic leaders. For followers of personalized charismatic leaders, self-worth becomes directly tied to the achievements of the leader. This is the personalized aspect of charisma manifested by leaders who claim to have unique power and an almost divine connection to what is true as long as everyone follows the leader blindly in word and deed.

During times of crisis, when personalized charismatic leadership is more likely to assert itself, these followers rely even more on the direction of the leader. As a result of suspending critical thought, these followers are able to rationalize even the most erratic leadership behavior. It is as if these followers have fallen under what Roberts and Bradley (1988) call a "magical spell" that manifests itself in an extreme form of loyalty to the leader.

There is also a danger to the personalized charismatic leader when follower support is unquestioned regardless of leadership behavior or results. The leader who is never challenged or questioned, regardless of their actions, can easily begin to feel a sense of unlimited power.

Without the normal checks and balances between leader behavior and follower support that guides almost all relationships, the leader can easily develop a type of God Complex and become more and more extreme in their actions due to believing that they will never lose the support of their core base of followers.

History is replete with examples of cult leaders and authoritarian leaders whose actions, no matter how extreme or abhorrent to the population at large, are accepted without question by their followers. Mass suicide, mass fraud, even mass murder are all accomplished only when a large group of followers participate with extreme loyalty in the actions and directions of the unethical leader.

The tendency for followers to overimitate the leader as well as place a disproportional amount of trust and faith in the leader can help explain the rise of charismatic leaders who do not adhere to the moral and ethical norms of the culture. Stutje (2012) describes the follower as experiencing a religious connection to the charismatic leader, attributing almost supernatural powers to the leader.

This willingness to follow the leader completely and without inhibition is a critical aspect of the personalized charismatic follower (Castelnovo, Popper, and Koren, 2017). In this relationship, the follower sees the charismatic leader as a kind of working-class hero. This dark side of charismatic leadership is only enhanced during times of great crisis or uncertainty.

Shamir, House, and Arthur (1993) describe the importance of the self-concept of the follower as critical to the followers' commitment to the charismatic leader. The followers' sense of self, of status, of belonging to a group is enhanced when there is an alignment between the followers' expectations and the leader's actions.

As the perceived value of the group is enhanced by words and actions of the charismatic leader, so too is the individual follower's sense of worth enhanced. When that follower sees the first followers filled with passion and purpose, the sense of worth only increases.

For many followers, the attraction to a specific leader and the assignment of charismatic affect to that leader is not based on the leader's message but rather on a very personal attachment to the leader as an idealized individual. This relationship, based on attraction to the person, not the message, is what House and Howell (1992) describe as a personalized relationship.

These followers of personalized charismatics may have low self-esteem. When individuals who are viewed as powerful, as rich, or who exhibit some other form of attractiveness, are seen to be speaking directly to the personalized follower, there is a strong likelihood that the follower can be directed to think, feel, and act in very specific ways, even if those influences are negative (Howell and Shamir, 2005).

Zablocki (1999) describes the personalized follower as having blind faith in the leader, resulting is a type of hypercompliance to the leader's direction. The potential the dark side of charisma has to be influenced by the behavior of the follower and the follower's blind acquiescence to the leader is as dangerous as the behavior of the leader (Conger, 1990; House and Howell, 1992; Howell and Avolio, 1992; Sankowsky, 1995; Howell and Shamir, 2005). In this view it is both parties that build the "dark side" of charisma.

The personalized follower is not particularly concerned with the leader's mission. The follower wants to be like the leader, however the leader is behaving or whatever the leader's message may be. As long as the leader is viewed by the follower as successful, as maintaining the attribute of success that the follower or group aspires to, the relationship and commitment to the leader will remain strong.

Personalized followers are also attracted to leaders who show great self-confidence. The more confident the leader acts and behaves, regardless of the outcomes, the better. Since follower approval is a given in this relationship, the leader may begin to feel unstoppable, as incapable of doing wrong, of making a mistake. In extreme settings, there is no action the leader can take, if taken with confidence, that the follower will not admire and support.

For the charismatic leader with personalized followers, the ability to influence the behaviors of followers can be extreme and the ability, or even the desire, of followers to influence the leader may be weak or nonexistent. The personalized follower does not want to change the leader, the personalized follower wants to be just like the leader. It is in these kinds of hyperpersonalized relationships that the dark side of charisma emerges.

The nature of the personalized charismatic, who is ego driven and sees him- or herself as the one and only key to success, makes it highly unlikely that an organization run by a personalized charismatic will evolve into a charismatic organization itself.

When personalized charismatics pass from the scene, either the mission of that charismatic leader will also fade or another personalized charismatic will attempt to step in and assume the mantel of leadership. This is often scene in cult-like organizations, where leadership transitions are often highly contentious.

Chapter Sixteen

All Together Now

INTRODUCTION

While this book has identified specific charismatic leadership attributes that are missing from the majority of licensing bodies, there is still a great deal of consensus regarding what good educational leadership looks like.

In addition to the standards identified by leadership scholars and state boards of education, policy makers, business leaders, parents, and other stakeholders also have working definitions of the skills that they look for in a leader. Each of these stakeholders operates with an internal definition of what it means to be a leader. Like art, the observer knows it when they see it.

The education leader can also be seen as the product of the specific identifiable attributes of charisma as discussed in this book. What best describes a charismatic leader versus other leadership descriptors is the summative nature of charismatic leadership attributes.

When examining the competencies identified by Zenger, Folkman, and other scholars, one can imagine a leader being successful without having full competency in every standard. For example, if there are sixteen competencies in the Zenger and Folkman leadership framework and a leader is highly competent in fourteen or fifteen of those competencies but is substandard in performance or skill set in one area, will that leader be ineffective? Probably not.

In most leadership frameworks there may be a hierarchy within the competencies themselves. Some leadership attributes have been shown to have a larger impact, when demonstrated consistently over time, than other leadership attributes.

For example, Zenger and Folkman (2002) found the standards that fall under the leadership category of interpersonal skills have more impact than the standards falling under the leadership category of personal capabilities.

They found that the leadership attribute of integrity/ethics stands alone as a prerequisite for all other leadership skills. Without the standard of integrity/ethics, the leader is incapable of sustaining success over time, even if the other leadership standards are being met.

This hierarchy of skills is not limited to leadership frameworks. Instructional frameworks such as those developed by Robert Marzano or Charlotte Danielson also subdivide the competencies identified for expert teaching by their impact. Certain pedagogical competencies are more critical for high-impact teaching and yield larger instructional results than other competencies.

The standards for charismatic leadership, however, are different. They are cumulative. For leaders to be seen as truly charismatic, they must demonstrate all the charismatic standards, not just a few or even most of them. That is not to say that there isn't great value in having leaders who can demonstrate energy, or confidence, or a mission focus. All of those attributes matter in and of themselves. They do not, however, independently yield a charismatic result.

IT ALL MATTERS

There is good news, however, regarding this all-or-nothing view of charisma and leadership. There is a kind of symbiotic relationship between all of the standards of charisma. As one standard is developed by the leader, it becomes easier, not harder, for the remaining standards to be achieved. There is a kind of charismatic momentum that occurs once leaders are able to develop and focus on a charismatic standard.

This cascading effect, where the last few charismatic standards are more likely to occur simply because the first few charismatic standards are occurring, paints a way forward for leaders wishing to benefit from the power of charisma or those who recruit, retain, and retrain leaders. Just as there are many more people in any organization who are capable of being leaders in the first place, there are also many more leaders in the organization who are capable of being charismatic leaders.

The tier 4 charismatic leader understands, and works on a daily basis, to develop the specific attributes of emotion, trust, competence, influence, energy, confidence, mission, and integrity/ethics. These eight attributes of the charismatic leader may at first appear overwhelming in scope and complexity. It is true that any one attribute is not necessarily common for all leaders to have, much less all of them.

All of these attributes are learnable and, as a result, can be developed. For the charismatic leader, the attributes are not a series of individual behaviors but one overarching and interdependent set of behaviors. As one attribute is developed, the remaining attributes become easier to develop. As one attribute occurs with regularity, it is more likely that the other attributes will also begin to occur on a regular basis.

A quick analysis of this interrelatedness of the charismatic attributes helps explain this phenomenon. For example, the attributes of integrity/ethics and trust complement each other. Trust is a primary building block for any impactful relationship between leaders and followers. Trust is also a critical component for any team that wishes to function at high levels and accomplish significant goals. For trust to occur, there must be an implied level of integrity and ethics between all parties. Once integrity is lost, so is trust. Once integrity is established, trust is likely to follow.

The charismatic attributes of mission, emotion, and energy are also interrelated. The goal to complete routine tasks does not generate significant amounts of emotion or energy for those assigned to complete the task.

On the other hand, missions that matter, missions that are bold and significant, will, in and of themselves, lead to an emotional response from those involved. If there is an emotional connection to the mission, then it is also much more likely that those involved will bring a significant amount of energy toward accomplishing the mission.

Finally, the attributes of competence, confidence, and influence are also linked. Skill sets and levels of expertise in any particular area, in other words the competence, to accomplish the mission at hand are directly correlated with the level of confidence that one has in the ability to accomplish the mission.

The higher the internal sense of competence that the leader has, the more external confidence the leader will be able to demonstrate. The charismatic leader is not hoping for success, the charismatic leader believes in success. That belief, manifested by an overwhelming sense of confidence in both the ability to accomplish the mission and the impact of the mission itself, is what establishes the leader's ability to influence others to also have that same belief in the mission, that same energy toward the mission, that same emotional response to the mission.

In fact, it is not hard to see the relationship between any of these attributes. We are all more likely to be influenced by those we trust. When a leader is not confident in the direction they are taking, it is unlikely that the leader will demonstrate a great deal of energy toward that particular set of goals. Without the energy to advocate for a particular position, it is less likely that the leader will be able to influence others toward that position.

There is no real end to the interdependence and interconnectedness of these charismatic attributes. That is good news for those seeking to harness the power of charisma as a critical leadership skill set.

It is this interdependence, this "all together now" nature of charismatic attributes that makes it possible for charisma to be developed and spread throughout the organization. There is a cause and effect that occurs with the development of charismatic leaders. The more that leaders focus on a subset of these attributes, the more success they will achieve in developing the remaining set of attributes.

Conversely, if leaders are not aware of, or interested in developing, these attributes, the likelihood that charismatic leadership will occur is extremely low. Charismatic leaders are not commonplace.

That rare charismatic leader is not, however, the result of predetermined leadership strengths possessed by a special small group of gifted individuals. Charismatic leadership attributes are teachable and learnable. If leadership potential is widely distributed throughout an organization, so too is the potential for charismatic leadership to emerge.

The fact that there are relatively few leaders who would be described by followers as charismatic says more about the processes and focus of leadership developers than of the potential for charismatic leadership to emerge from any dedicated group or team. Charisma, the fourth tier of modern educational leadership, is the next logical step for the development of the leader on a mission that matters most—making a difference in the lives of all children.

Bibliography

Ammons, D. N., and C. Newell. (1989). *City Executives: Leadership Roles, Work Characteristics, and Time Management.* Albany: SUNY Press.

Antonakis, J., N. Bastardoz, P. Jacquart, and B. Shamir. (2016). "Charisma: An Ill-defined and Ill-measured Gift." *Annual Review of Organizational Psychology and Organizational Behavior* 3(1): 293–319.

Antonakis, J., M. Fenley, and S. Liechti. (2011). "Can Charisma Be Taught? Tests of Two Interventions." *Academy of Management Learning & Education* 10(3): 374–96.

Aragon, S. (2016). "Teacher Shortages: What We Know." Teacher Shortage Series. *Education Commission of the States.*

Ashforth, B. E., and G. E. Kreiner. (2002). "Normalizing Emotion in Organizations: Making the Extraordinary Seem Ordinary." *Human Resource Management Review* 12(2): 215–35.

Askins, K. (2009). "'That's Just What I Do': Placing Emotion in Academic Activism." *Emotion, Space and Society* 2(1): 4–13.

Atwater, L., and A. Carmeli. (2009). "Leader-Member Exchange, Feelings of Energy and Involvement in Creative Work." *The Leadership Quarterly* 20(3): 264–75.

Avolio, B. J., R. J. Reichard, S. T. Hannah, F. O. Walumbwa, and A. Chan. (2009). "A Meta-Analytic Review of Leadership Impact Research: Experimental and Quasi-Experimental Studies." *The Leadership Quarterly* 20: 764–84.

Avolio, B. J., and F. Yammarino. (2013). *Introduction to, and Overview of, Transformational and Charismatic Leadership.* Bingley, West Yorkshire, England: Emerald Group Publishing Limited.

Awamleh, R., and W. L. Gardner. (1999). "Perceptions of Leader Charisma and Effectiveness: The Effects of Vision, Content, Delivery and Organizational Performance." *The Leadership Quarterly* 10(3): 345–73.

Aziri, B. (2011). "Job Satisfaction: A Literature Review." *Management Research and Practice* 3(4).

Bandura, A. (1993). "Perceived Self-Efficacy in Cognitive Development and Functioning." *Educational Psychologist* 28(2): 117–48.

Banks, C. B., K. N. Engemann, C. E. Williams, J. Gooty, K. D. McCauley, and M. R. Medaugh. (2017). "A Meta-analytic Review and Future Research Agenda of Charismatic Leadership." *The Leadership Quarterly* 28: 508–29.

Barnett, K., and J. McCormick. (2004). "Leadership and Individual Principal-Teacher Relationships in Schools." *Educational Administration Quarterly* 40(3): 406–34.

Bass, B. M. (1985). *Leadership and Performance beyond Expectations*. New York: The Free Press.

Bass, B. M., and B. J. Avolio. (1989). "Potential Biases in Leadership Measures: How Prototypes, Leniency, and General Satisfaction Relate to Ratings and Rankings of Transformational and Transactional Leadership Constructs." *Educational and Psychology Measurement* 49(3).

Bennett, N., and J. Lemoine. (2014). "What a Difference a Word Makes: Understanding Threats to Performance in a VUCA World." *Business Horizons* 57(3): 311–17.

Bennis, W. (1999). "The Leadership Advantage." *Leader to Leader* 12(2): 18–23.

Betancourt, S. (September 2018). "Teacher Shortages Worsening in Majority of US States, Study Reveals." Retrieved from www.theguardian.com.

Beteille, T., D. Kalogrides, and S. Loeb. (2012). "Stepping Stones: Principal Career Paths and School Outcomes." *Social Science Research* 41(4): 904–19.

Bligh, M. C., C. L. Pearce, and J. C. Kohles. (2006). "The Importance of Self and Shared Leadership in Team Based Knowledge Work: A Meso-Level Model of Leadership Dynamics." *Journal of Managerial Psychology* 21(4): 296–318.

Bromley, H., and V. Kirschner-Bromley. (2007). "Are You a Transformational Leader?" *Physician Executive* 33(6): 54–57.

Burns, J. M. (1978). *Leadership*. New York: Harper & Row.

Caruso, D. R., and P. Salovey. (2004). *The Emotionally Intelligent Manager: How to Develop and Use the Four Key Emotional Skills of Leadership*. Hoboken, NJ: John Wiley & Sons.

Castelnovo, O., M. Popper, and D. Koren. (2017). "The Innate Code of Charisma." *The Leadership Quarterly* 28: 543–54.

CBS News: *Moneywatch*. (April 2, 2018). "Advertisers Bail as Laura Ingraham Goes on Vacation."

Choi, J. (2006). "A Motivational Theory of Charismatic Leadership: Envisioning, Empathy, and Empowerment." *Journal of Leadership & Organizational Studies* 13(1): 24–43.

Churms, S. (November 11, 2016). Principal Intern Reflection #3. Volusia County, Florida.

Ciulla, J. B. (2004). "Ethics and Leadership Effectiveness." In *The Nature of Leadership*, Antondas, J., Cianciola, A., Sternberg, B. (eds.), 302–27 Thousand Oaks, CA: Sage.

Cohen, A. (2015). *Two-Dimensional Man: An Essay on the Anthropology of Power and Symbolism in Complex Society*. Routledge.

Colwell, C. (2018). *Mission-Driven Leadership: Understanding the Challenges Facing Schools Today*. Lanham, MD: Rowman & Littlefield.

Conger, J. (1990). "The Dark Side of Leadership." *Organizational Dynamics* 19(2): 42–55.

Conger, J. (2015). *Charismatic Leadership*, Volume 11. Hoboken, NJ: John Wiley & Sons.

Conger, J. A., and R. N. Kanungo. (1988). "Behavioral Dimensions of Charismatic Leadership." *Journal of Management* 15(2): 1989.

Conger, J. A., R. N. Kanungo, and S. T. Menon. (2000). "Charismatic Leadership and Follower Effects." *Journal of Organizational Behavior* 21(7): 747–67.

Cooper, R. K., and A. Sawaf. (1998). *Executive EQ: Emotional Intelligence in Leadership and Organizations*. New York: Penguin.

Costello, B., J. Wachtel, and T. Wachtel. (2009). *The Restorative Practices Handbook: For Teachers, Disciplinarians and Administrators.* Bethlehem, PA: International Institute for Restorative Practices.

Covey, S. R. (1989). *The 7 Habits of Highly Effective People: Restoring the Character Ethic* ([rev. ed.]). New York: Free Press.

Dawson, L. L. (2011). "Charismatic Leadership in Millennial Movements." In *Oxford Handbook of Millennialism*. Oxford, UK: Oxford University Press.

DeGroot, T., D. S. Kiker, and T. C. Cross. (2001). "A Meta-Analysis to Review Organizational Outcomes Related to Charismatic Leadership." *Canadian Journal of Administrative Sciences* 17(4): 356–71.

DePree, M. (1990). *Leadership Is an Art*. New York: Dell.

Dollard, M. F., and J. C. Metzer. (1999). "Psychological Research, Practice, and Production: The Occupational Stress Problem." *International Journal of Stress Management* 6(4): 241–53.

DuFour, R. (2002). "The Learning-Centered Principal." *Educational Leadership* 59(8): 12–15.

Edwards, J. R., R. D. Caplan, and R. Van Harrison. (1998). "Person-Environment Fit Theory." *Theories of Organizational Stress* 28: 67.

Everard, K. B., G. Morris, and I. Wilson. (2004). *Effective School Management*. Thousand Oaks, CA: Sage.

Fogleman, R. R. (2001). "The Leadership-Integrity Link." *Concepts for Air Force Leadership*: 39–40. Maxwell AFB, AL: Air University Press.

Friedland, W. H. (1964). "For a Sociological Concept of Charisma." *Social Forces* 43(1): 18–26.

Gardner, W. (2003). "Perceptions of Leader Charisma, Effectiveness, and Integrity: Effects of Exemplification, Delivery, and Ethical Reputation." *Management Communication Quarterly* 16(4): 502–27.

Gibson, S., and M. H. Dembo. (1984). "Teacher Efficacy: A Construct Validation." *Journal of Educational Psychology* 76(4): 569–82.

Gillespie, N. A., and L. Mann. (2004). "Transformational Leadership and Shared Values: The Building Blocks of Trust." *Journal of Managerial Psychology*.

Goddard, R. D., W. K. Hoy, and A. Woolfolk Hoy. (2000). "Collective Teacher Efficacy: Its Meaning, Measure, and Impact on Student Achievement." *American Educational Research Journal* 37(2): 479–507.

Grabo, A., B. Spisak, and M. van Vugt. (2017). "Charisma as Signal: An Evolutionary Perspective on Charismatic Leadership." *The Leadership Quarterly* 28: 473–85.

Graham, J. W. (1995). "Leadership, Moral Development, and Citizenship Behavior." *Business Ethics Quarterly* 5(1): 43–54.

Hackman, M., and C. Johnson. (1991). *Leadership*. Prospect Heights, IL: Waveland Press.

Hall, K., R. Croom, and L. Hancock. (2019). "Thriving, Embeddedness, and Connection: Data, Theory and Practice." Stetson University Academic Leaders Retreat.

Harris, A. (2003). "Teacher Leadership as Distributed Leadership: Heresy, Fantasy or Possibility?" *School Leadership and Management* 23(3): 313–24.

Haslam, S. A., S. D. Reicher, and M. J. Platow. (2010). *The New Psychology of Leadership: Identity, Influence, and Power*. London: Psychology Press.

Hesselbein, F., and E. K. Shinseki. (2004). "Be. Know. Do." Adapted from the official US Army leadership manual *Leadership the Army Way*.

House, R. J. (1977). "A Theory of Leadership Effectiveness." In J. G. Hunt and L. L. Larson (eds.), *Leadership: The Cutting Edge*, 189–207. Carbondale: Southern Illinois Press.

House R. J., and J. Howell. (1992). "Personality and Charismatic Leadership." *Leadership Quarterly* 3: 81–108.

Howell, J., and B. Avolio. (1992). "The Ethics of Charismatic Leadership: Submission or Liberation?" *Academy of Management Executive* 6(2): 43–54.

Howell, J., and B. Shamir. (2005). "The Role of Followers in the Charismatic Leadership Process: Relationships and Their Consequences." *The Academy of Management Review* 30(1): 96–112.

Huber, S. G., and D. Muijs. (2010). "School Leadership Effectiveness: The Growing Insight in the Importance of School Leadership for the Quality and Development of Schools and Their Pupils." In S. G. Huber (ed.), *School Leadership—International Perspectives*, 57–77. Dordecht: Springer.

Joosse, P. (2017). "Max Weber's Disciples: Theorizing the Charismatic Aristocracy." *Sociological Theory* 35(4): 334–58.

Judge, T. A., and R. F. Piccolo. (2004). "Transformational and Transactional Leadership: A Meta-Analytic Test of Their Relative Validity." *Journal of Applied Psychology* 89(5): 755–68.

Katz, Y. (2017). *The Relationship between Teacher's Perceptions of Emotional Labour, Teacher Burnout, and Teachers' Educational Level*. Presentation given at the Nineteenth Annual International Conference on Education, Athens, Greece.

Kelly, R. C., B. Thornton, and R. Daugherty. (2005). "Relationships between Measures of Leadership and School Climate." *Education 313: International Journal of Primary, Elementary and Early Years Education* 126(1): 17.

Kennedy, J. F. (1962). *State of the Union Address*. US Army Transportation School.

Kets de Vries, M. (1988). "Prisoners of Leadership." *Human Relations* 41(31): 261–80.

Keyes, C. F. (2002). "Weber and Anthropology." *Annual Review of Anthropology* 31: 233–55.

Kiisel, T. (2013). "Without It, No Real Success Is Possible." Forbes.com

Kirp, D. (September 3, 2017). "Don't Suspend Students. Empathize." *New York Times*, p. SR3.

Kohut, H. (1978). *The Search for the Self*. New York: International University Press.

Korosec, K. (2014). *The One Asterisk on Tesla's Patent Giveaway*. www.Fortune.com

Kouzes, J. M., and B. Z. Posner. (2010). *The Truth about Leadership*. Soundview Executive Book Summaries. Hoboken, NJ: John Wiley & Sons.

Ladkin, D., and S. Taylor. (2010). "Enacting the 'True Self': Towards a Theory of Embodied Authentic Leadership." *The Leadership Quarterly* 21(1): 64–74.

Leithwood, K., and D. Jantzi. (2000). "The Effects of Transformational Leadership on Organizational Conditions and Student Engagement with School." *Journal of Educational Administration*.

Levin, S., and K. Bradley. (2019). "Understanding and Addressing Principal Turnover: A Review of the Research." Reston, VA: National Association of Secondary School Principals.

Liebig, J. E. (1991). *Business Ethics: Profiles in Civic Virtue*. Fulcrum Publishing, 134–35.

Maclachlan, B. (1996). *The Age of Grace: Charis in Early Greek Poetry*. Princeton, NJ: Princeton University Press.

Mayer, J. D., P. Salovey, and D. Sluyter. (1997). "Emotional Development and Emotional Intelligence: Implications for Educators." *What Is Emotional Intelligence*: 3–31.

Merriam Webster Online. Retrieved August 7, 2019, from www.merriam-webster.com/dictionalry/citation. Volatility [Def.1]. (n.d.). Merriam-Webster Online.

Middleton, K. L. (2005). "The Service-Learning Project as a Supportive Context for Charismatic Leadership Emergence in Nascent Leaders." *Academy of Management Learning & Education* 4(3): 295–308.

Miller, J. B., and I. P. Stiver. (1997). *The Healing Connection: How Women Form Relationships in Therapy and in Life*. Boston, MA: Beacon Press.

Northouse, P. G. (2018). *Leadership: Theory and Practice* (eighth ed.). Thousand Oaks, CA: Sage Publications.

Ofori, G. (2009). "Ethical Leadership: Examining the Relationships with Full-Range Leadership Model, Employee Outcomes, and Organizational Culture." *Journal of Business Ethics* 90(4): 533.

Ostroff, C., and T. J. Rothausen. (1997). "The Moderating Effect of Tenure in Person-Environment Fit: A Field Study in Educational Organizations." *Journal of Occupational and Organizational Psychology* 70(2): 173–88.

Papa, F. C., H. Lankford, and J. Wyckoff. (2002). "The Attributes and Career Paths of Principals: Implications for Improving Policy." Teacher Policy Research Center.

Pearce, C. L., J. E. Hoch, H. J. Jeppesen, and J. Wegge. (2010). "New Forms of Management." *Personnel Psychology* 9: 151–153.

Pijanowski, J. C., P. M. Hewitt, and K. P. Brady. (2009). "Superintendents' Perceptions of the Principal Shortage." *NASSP Bulletin* 93(2): 85–95.

Pink, D. H. (2012). *To Sell Is Human: The Surprising Truth about Moving Others*. New York: Riverhead Books.

Plutchik, R. (1994). *The Psychology and Biology of Emotion*. New York: Harper-Collins College Publishers.

Popper, M. (2014). "Why Do People Follow?" In L. Lapierre and M. Carsten (eds.), *Followership: What Is It and Why Do People Follow?* Bingley, UK: Emerald.

Porath, C., G. Spreitzer, C. Gibson, and F. G. Garnett. (2012). "Thriving at Work: Toward Its Measurement, Construct Validation, and Theoretical Refinement." *Journal of Organizational Behavior* 33(2): 250–75.

Professional Standards for Educational Administration. (2015). Reston, VA.

Quinn, R. E. (2004). *Building the Bridge As You Walk on It: A Guide for Leading Change* (Vol. 204). Hoboken, NJ: John Wiley & Sons.

Reiss, R. (September 11, 2017). "Top CEOs Place High Value on Corporate Ethics and Social Responsibility to Drive Business." *Forbes*.

Rhoades, L., and R. Eisenberger. (2002). "Perceived Organizational Support: A Review of the Literature." *Journal of Applied Psychology* 87: 698–714.

Robbins, S. P. (1998). *Organizational Behavior*. Upper Saddle River, NJ: Prentice Hall.

Roberts, N. C., and R. T. Bradley. (1988). *Charismatic Leadership: The Elusive Factor in Organizational Effectiveness*. San Francisco: Jossey-Bass.

RoBnagel, C. S. (2017). "Leadership and Motivation." In *Leadership Today*, edited by J. Marques and S. Dhiman. Springer Texts in Business and Economics.

Rousmaniere, K. (2013). *The Principal's Office: A Social History of the American School Principal*. Albany: State University of New York Press.

Russell, J. L., and L. L. Sabina. (2014). "Planning for Principal Succession." *Journal of School Leadership* 24: 599–634.

Ryff, C. D., and B. Singer (eds.). (2001). *Emotion, Social Relationships and Health*. New York: Oxford University Press, USA.

Sabina, L. (2014). *Factors Influencing Elements of Stress and Autonomy and Control among School Administrators* (Doctoral dissertation, University of Pittsburgh).

Sabina, L. L., and C. Colwell. (2018). "Challenges of Principal Succession: Examining the Challenges of Hiring Internal vs. External Candidates." *Athens Journal of Education* 5(4): 375–395.

Sabina, L. L., and C. Colwell. (2020). "Leadership Attributes and State Standards." *Southeast Journal of Educational Administration*.

Salovey, P., and J. Mayer. (1990). "Emotional Intelligence." *Sage Publications* 9(3): 185–211.

Sankowsky, D. (1995). "The Charismatic Leader as Narcissist: Understanding the Abuse of Power." *Organizational Dynamics* 23(4): 57–71.

Schjoedt, U., J. Sorensen, K. Nieblo, D. Xygalatas, P. Mitkidis, and J. Bulbulia. (2013). "Cognitive Resonance Depletion in Religious Interactions." *Religion, Brain & Behavior* 3(1): 39–55.

Schneider, M., and M. Somers. (2006). "Organizations as Complex Adaptive Systems: Implications of Complexity Theory for Leadership Research." *The Leadership Quarterly* 17(4): 351–65.

Scribner, J. P., R. K. Sawyer, S. T. Watson, and V. L. Myers. (2007). "Teacher Teams and Distributed Leadership: A Study of Group Discourse and Collaboration." *Educational Administration Quarterly* 43(1): 67–100.

Senge, P. M. (2006). *The Fifth Discipline: The Art and Practice of the Learning Organization.* New York: Broadway Business.

Shamir, B., R. J. House, and M. B. Arthur. (1993). "The Motivational Effects of Charismatic Leadership: A Self-Concept Based Theory." *Organizational Science* 4: 577–93.

Silvia, P. J., and R. E. Beaty. (2012). "Making Creative Metaphors: The Importance of Fluid Intelligence for Creative Thought." *Intelligence* 40(4): 343–51.

Spreitzer, G. (1995). "Psychological Empowerment in the Workplace: Dimensions, Measurement, and Validation." *Academy of Management Journal* 38: 1442–65.

Spreitzer, G., K. Sutcliffe, J. Dutton, S. Sonenshein, and A. M. Grant. (2005). "A Socially Embedded Model of Thriving at Work." *Organization Science* 16(5): 537–49.

Stahl, L. (writer). (December 9, 2018). Elon Musk. [Television series episode] In L. Stahl (producer), *60 Minutes*, CBS Network.

Stallard, M. L. (April 9, 2016). "Leading with Character: Integrity." www.michael leestallard.com

Stutje, J. W. (2012). *Charismatic Leadership and Social Movements: The Revolutionary Power of Ordinary Men and Women.* New York: Berghahn Books.

Superville, D. (May 2018). "How Long Do Big-City Superintendents Actually Last?" Retrieved from www.educationnweek.com.

Sutcher, L., L. Darling-Hammond, and D. Carver-Thomas. (2016). "A Coming Crisis in Teaching? Teacher Supply, Demand, and Shortages in the U.S." Learning Policy Institute.

Thessin, R. (2017). *Superintendent Transition Teams.* UCEA Conference, Seattle, Washington.

Tomasello, M., and H. Rakoczy. (2003). "What Makes Human Cognition Unique? From Individual to Shared Collective Intentionality." *Mind and Language* 18: 121–47.

Tschannen-Moran, M. (2009). "Fostering Teacher Professionalism in Schools: The Role of Leadership and Trust." *Educational Administration Quarterly*.

Tschannen-Moran, M. (2014). *Trust Matters: Leadership for Successful Schools.* Hoboken, NJ: John Wiley & Sons.

Tucker, R. C. (1970). In *The Theory of Charismatic Authority*, edited by D. A. Rustow. Philosophers and Kings Studies in Leadership. New York: George Braziller.

Turner, B. A. (ed.). (2014). *Organizational Symbolism* (Vol. 19). Walter de Gruyter.

Van Dierendonck, D. (2011). "Servant Leadership: A Review and Synthesis." *Journal of Management* 37(4): 1228–61.

Van Maanen, J., E. H. Schein, and B. M. Staw. (1979). *Research in Organizational Behavior.* BM Staw (ed.). (1): 209–64. Greenwich, CT: JAI Press.

Volatility. (n.d.). In *Merriam-Webster's Collegiate Dictionary*. Retrieved from www .meriam-webster.com/dictionary/volatility.

Weber, M. (1946). In H. Gerth and C. Wright Mills (eds.), *Max Weber: Essays in Sociology*. New York: Oxford University Press.

Weber, M. (1947). In A. M. Henderson and T. Parsons (eds.), *The Theory of Social and Economic Organization*. New York: Oxford University Press Trans.

Weber, M. (1968). *On Charisma and Institutional Building*. Chicago: Chicago University Press.

Wing Institute. (May 2019). "The Wing Institute: What Is the Turnover Rate for School Principals?" Retrieved from www.winginstitute.org.

Zablocki, B. (1999). "Hyper-Compliance in Charismatic Groups." In D. D. Franks and T. S. Thomas (eds.), *Mind, Brain, and Society: Toward a Neurosociology of Emotion*, 287–310. Stanford, CT: JAI Press.

Zenger, J., and J. Folkman. (2002). *The Extraordinary Leader: Turning Good Managers into Great Leaders*. New York: McGraw Hill.

Zenger, J., and J. Folkman. (February 2019). "The 3 Elements of Trust." *Harvard Business Review*.

About the Author

Chris Colwell, EdD, is an associate professor and chair of the Education Department at Stetson University in Deland, Florida. Dr. Colwell teaches teacher education and educational leadership education and serves as a consultant on P–12 leadership development. His research interests focus primarily on school leadership. He draws from forty years of work as a classroom teacher, an assistant principal, a principal at all levels of P–12 education, and a deputy superintendent prior to joining Stetson University. Chris was named the Secondary Principal of the Year for the state of Florida. He served as president of the Florida Organization of Instructional Leaders during his tenure as a deputy superintendent for Instructional Services for the Volusia County, Florida, School District. Chris is the author of the books *Impact: How Assistant Principals Can Be High Performing Leaders*, published by Rowman & Littlefield in 2015, and *Mission-Driven Leadership: Understanding the Challenges Facing Schools Today*, published by Rowman & Littlefield in 2018.